GROWING CHURCH LEADERS

NEW Skills For New Tasks

ROBERT H. RAMEY, JR.

PRESS

CTS Press
Copyright ©1995 CTS Press
Book design by Melissa Mahoney

ISBN 1-885121-13-X

CTS Press
P.O. Box 520
Decatur, GA 30031

GROWING CHURCH LEADERS

New Skills For New Tasks

ROBERT H. RAMEY, JR.

To A. Chalmers Hope –
wise physician,
dedicated elder,
and
warm friend.

"How can I grow as a church leader?" If you have ever asked yourself that question, this book may help you. Too often churches prepare leaders for jobs, for "business as usual" – leading them onto the programmatic merry-go-round and ultimately leaving them "burned out" and unfulfilled. Yet preparing persons for leadership only begins a process that must be maintained if the church is to be renewed – especially to meet the challenges of a new day.

Now more than ever we must nurture church leaders, since the church, as I see it, stands on a new "missionary" plain that requires us to view the world differently. The Constantinian or Establishment Church, so long propped up by the prevailing culture, is either dead or gasping for breath almost everywhere – and in the midst of its collapse we must learn new ways to function as church leaders.

Indeed, I am convinced that the decline of mainline churches will force future church leaders to function differently. Leadership education for our new situation draws deeply and liberally from scripture. Indeed, one can trace many of the problems in today's church to its frequent abandonment of scriptural roots. Thus I suggest that we reexamine both qualifications for leaders in the early church – which stood on a similar "missionary plain" – and the source of their astonishing power.

I believe lay leaders today hunger for a deeper Christian experience and that spiritually growing leaders can face the challenge of today's world. Moreover, the present crisis challenges laypersons to take up the mantle of leadership designed for them and to join with ministers in discernment and faith to lead the church in a new day.

I envision that ministers will lead their boards in a study of this book – perhaps assigning a chapter to be discussed at each meeting, using the questions at the end of each chapter to initiate discussion. Or, leaders may decide to conduct an in-depth study during a retreat, employing the suggestions in Appendix A for a spirituality retreat, or the suggestions in Appendix B for developing collaborative skills, or the suggestions in Appendix D as the content for special quarterly meetings. So used, these ideas will equip laypersons to deepen their faith and knowledge and become more effective in serving a changing world.

While scripture forms the platform for this emphasis, I also draw freely upon other resources congruent with the faith and life of the church. I have learned much from the management theories of Rensis Likert, as well as from Paul Dietterich and colleagues at the Center for Parish Development in Chicago. The Alban Institute in Washington has also informed my work. The pioneering efforts of James Hopewell in the field of congregational studies have further helped me. Moreover, the influence of writers like Paul Minear, Robert K. Greenleaf, John B. Cobb, Jr., Edwin H. Friedman, Douglas John Hall, Jackson W. Carroll, Carl S. Dudley, Roy S. Oswald, Loren Mead, Speed B. Leas, Alvin Lindgren, Norman Shawchuck, Roger Heuser, and Kennon L. Callahan will readily be seen in my approach to leadership development.

Church leaders in my five pastorates plus participants in numerous workshops have helped me gain many insights. Even as I thank them, I want to thank Ben Campbell Johnson for reading my manuscript and making helpful suggestions. Nancy Graham, editor at CTS Press, is due my deep gratitude for her painstaking work in editing the manuscript. Also, I am particularly grateful to C. Benton Kline, Jr., who once again proved that his wise counsel both saves authors from making foolish mistakes while providing enough encouragement for them to persevere! Finally, I would be remiss not to thank the Board of Trustees of Columbia Theological Seminary for giving me a sabbatical leave to complete this project.

May God bless you and the whole church as together we step boldly onto a new frontier.

ROBERT H. RAMEY, JR.

Serving to Lead

The Christian church stands at a crossroads today. The contemporary context in which we do ministry has radically changed. The cry for leadership has never been more urgent. Our routine way of selecting and installing leaders proves inadequate for the challenge in which we find ourselves. This strong appeal for dynamic leadership is not intended to intimidate the new leader or disparage the experienced one, but rather to stress how crucial training, discipline, and development really are for today's leaders.

Our approach to leadership development reaches beyond the routine criteria for the selection of leaders. By looking again at the text of scripture, we find new inspiration and guidance for this task.

Everyone who accepts a leadership role intends to do a good job, to reach others, to perform effectively. This book aims to help you do all these things as you recognize the demands of leadership in a new day.

Minister, elder, deacon, member of the vestry or administrative council, committee moderator, mission team coordinator – whatever your position, you play a crucial role!

By committing yourself to serve, you help shape both the governance and the spiritual direction of your congregation and, less directly, the whole Christian movement. And that is an amazing opportunity.

WHY PEOPLE ARE INVITED TO LEADERSHIP

Frankly, multiple factors influence persons nominating others for church leadership. We often lean toward men and women regarded as "successful" – who possess power, wealth, or prestige. We may recognize a nominee's commitment to important causes or civic organizations, popularity within the congregation, faithful church attendance, clear business acumen, pleasant demeanor, or leadership skills.

These natural attributes of leadership and commitment can certainly prove valuable. Indeed, the early church considered natural leadership qualities important when selecting elders.[1] And of course, being a natural community leader should not disqualify a person from a church leadership position.

Certainly many congregations, upon further reflection, value the character of their leaders rather than functional "qualifications." When training church leaders in various workshops, I often ask groups, "Who are the best church leaders you have ever known? What were they like?" Descriptions from one workshop included:

- caring
- understanding
- humble
- set good example
- committed
- love of Jesus as Savior and Lord
- forgiving
- loving
- listened well
- accepting
- wise

While this list may not clearly identify all the spiritual roots of leadership, it reveals the fruits of a vital relationship with Jesus Christ.

Still, most congregations would plead guilty to neglecting biblical norms when choosing leaders. Because we are unabashedly Christian leaders, however, and not generic community leaders, we must lift our pattern for selecting Christian leadership from scripture. And today, as our cultural situation more closely parallels that of the first century church, we may draw particular insights from the witness of those earliest church leaders and from Jesus himself.

The book of Acts recounts the efforts and experiences of the early church, revealing seven qualifications for leadership.

1) Christian leaders are called to office by God through Jesus Christ. After the ascension of Jesus, Peter exhorted the company of one hundred and twenty to choose a replacement for Judas. They put forth two men, Joseph called Barsabbas, and Matthias, and they prayed for guidance: "Lord, you know everyone's heart. Show us which one of these two *you have chosen* to take the place in this ministry and apostleship from which Judas turned aside to go to his own place" (Acts 1:24, 25, italics mine).

The group of one hundred and twenty then cast lots and chose Matthias. To most of us, casting lots seems an odd – and maybe even unspiritual – way to choose a leader; yet, importantly, they strongly believed that *God* had chosen Matthias. Notice the crucial dimension of this story: the leaders sought God's will. We might learn from them, since we sometimes neglect the obvious.

2) Christian leaders possess a Christian experience. Though Acts does not use these exact words, the fact remains. Peter urged the one hundred and twenty to choose "one of the men who have *accompanied* us during all the time that the Lord Jesus went in and out among us...one of these must become a witness with us to his resurrection" (Acts 1:21,22, italics mine). Thus Christian leaders have a firsthand, personal relationship with Jesus Christ. While it's impossible for today's Christian leaders literally to have been with Jesus in the flesh and to have witnessed his resurrection, we can experience him in the Spirit and live the Christian life on the basis of this inner reality. Is it not essential for us to say also, "We have been with Jesus. We have experienced his amazing grace"?

3) Christian leaders bear witness to the Christian message, especially the resurrection. The early Christian leaders preached the whole gospel, from Jesus' fulfillment of prophecy to his second coming. At the heart of their message was the resurrection. Without the resurrection they would not have preached at all. Because of the resurrection, the company of believers selected Matthias to join the other apostles to witness to this cornerstone event.

Even the leaders appointed under the apostles to "wait on tables" (Acts 6:2) extended their service to proclaiming the gospel with power. Stephen did this (Acts 7) and so did Philip (Acts 8:4-13, 26-40) – preaching the full Christian message and emphasizing the resurrection.

Over and over again the first Christian preachers said with Peter, "This Jesus God raised up, and of that all of us are witnesses" (Acts 2:32). Those leaders knew that without belief in the resurrection the young church would collapse like a house built on sand. So will today's church.

4) Christian leaders are empowered by the Holy Spirit. The first Christian leaders could not have witnessed in power without the gift of the Holy Spirit. Jesus had already promised, "But you will receive power when the Holy Spirit has come upon you; and you will be my witnesses in Jerusalem, in all Judea and Samaria, and to the ends of the earth" (Acts 1:8). God poured out that power at Pentecost.

When Peter charged the whole community of disciples to select the seven to wait on tables, he urged them to pick men "full of the Spirit" (Acts 6:3). The faithful encourager, Barnabas, was said to be "a good man, *full of the Holy Spirit* and of faith" (Acts 11:24, italics mine). At Ephesus Paul told the Ephesian elders to keep watch over themselves and their flock "of which the *Holy Spirit* has made you overseers" (Acts 20:28, italics mine). Without the Holy Spirit the first Christian leaders would have been powerless.

Often those of us in today's church do not lean on the Holy Spirit as we should, perhaps only calling on the Spirit when we grow desperate. What's more, we often fall into an activities trap, as though to justify ourselves by the number of programs we offer. Perhaps we can find new energy and joy by realizing that the Holy Spirit drives the church: not bottom lines, quotas, rugged individualism, or human effort alone. Cannot today's leaders be filled with the Holy Spirit?

5) Christian leaders serve as examples of Christian faith. Luke implies throughout his narrative that leaders were expected to live what they taught. Thus Peter urged the community of believers to choose men "*of good standing*" (Acts 6:3, italics mine) to serve. Stephen performed signs and wonders among the people of Jerusalem and embodied forgiveness when he prayed for his killers (Acts 7:60). And certainly Peter and Paul repeatedly demonstrated the faith they preached throughout the Mediterranean world. The early leaders were persons of faith, who lived the Christian life with courage and conviction every day.

While they will never be sinless, increasingly the leaders we select should be persons saved from their sin, by grace, through their faith in Jesus Christ.

6) Christian leaders should receive the approval of the Christian community before they serve. In Jerusalem the whole community of disciples picked seven, whom the apostles affirmed and prayed for (Acts 6:6), for ministry of service. Paul and Barnabas appointed elders in church after church on their missionary journeys. And while we can't be sure the churches voted for elders, the word "appoint" means literally "choose by the show of hands" and implies some kind of popular voting. Even Paul himself required the approval and support of Ananias and the disciples at Damascus (Acts 9:1-25). So some Christian group, whether church or apostles or the one hundred and twenty, approved persons for office. The early leaders did not simply rise up individually and start serving the church as leaders.

The church must still confirm a leader's call to serve. The corporate nature of the church is a crucial part of the biblical witness. It has never been sufficient for a person, acting alone, to assume a call to leadership in the church. The secret or "inner call" to lead must be confirmed by the community of faith. Most denominations do not ordain laity to leadership positions as do Presbyterian churches, but leaders in all denominations are chosen and installed by some method.

7) Christian leaders serve in order to lead. Here we shift from Luke's narrative in Acts to Luke's Gospel, where we read that after the Last Supper an argument broke out among the disciples concerning who was the greatest. "The greatest among you must become like the youngest," Jesus admonished, "and the leader like one who serves" (Lk. 22:26). So if you want to be a leader in the kingdom of God, Jesus sets forth the primary qualification: service. Serving others, not lording it over them as some leaders do (Lk. 22:25).

In the same table discussion Jesus said, "I am among you as one who serves" (Lk. 22:27). Interestingly, he did what the apostles decided in Acts they did not have time to do – wait on tables! On another occasion (Jn. 13:1-20), Jesus stooped to wash the disciples' feet, an act they would not stoop to perform. So in word and deed, from the beginning of his ministry to the end, Jesus took the form of a servant.

The servant image itself is drawn from the Servant Songs of Isaiah, in particular Isaiah 52:13-53:12. Here the suffering servant hurts vicariously for others. To a remarkable degree Jesus fulfilled Isaiah's prophecy. With his stripes we are healed through the cross.

Who can doubt that Jesus intended to become such a suffering servant?

The entire New Testament confirms that Jesus came not to be served but to serve. And so should it be for anyone who desires to be a church leader. "For to this you have been called," wrote Peter in powerful echoes of Isaiah 53, "because Christ also suffered for you, leaving you an example, so that you should follow in his steps" (1 Pet. 2:21).

The witness of scripture about servanthood can hardly be stronger or more apparent, yet we still argue about greatness. It's almost as though we had never read this story. Do not Jesus' words and examples indisputably teach us that leadership in the kingdom must be based on service, even waiting on tables? Perhaps he needs to come and sit down with us as he did with his disciples long ago and say, "Haven't you learned yet? Greatness is found in service, not power; service, not prestige; service, not possessions." And if the desire to serve is not our fundamental reason for being and leading, we should not lead. It's just that simple – and difficult!

PULLING IT ALL TOGETHER

God calls leaders to help pilot the church in Spirit-led fashion toward Spirit-designed goals and challenges. As a Christian leader, this is your calling.

The call challenges us not merely to maintain faith in the midst of responsibilities but to grow in faith – and to help the church grow in faith as well. Leadership renewal begins when we emphasize both biblical qualifications for church leadership and growth in grace while serving.

Christian leaders today must model a vital relationship with our Triune God and nurture that relationship while serving. The church has failed to do both tasks adequately, although we have proved especially weak in nurturing the ongoing relationship of leaders while they serve. That task gets lost in the midst of reading financial reports, purchasing paper clips, and resolving staff conflicts.

Simply put, the church can never meet the challenges of the 21st century unless its leaders are growing in faith and the life of discipleship. To march aggressively into a new era, we must become a community of persons in Christ. A grounding in a vital community informs everything church leaders do.

Questions for Discussion

1. How have leaders been selected in your church? What criteria has governed their selection? How are biblical criteria considered?

2. What do you understand as "a Christian experience"? How important is it for Christian leaders to possess a Christian experience? What effect does it have on the church when they do not?

3. What evidence do you see in your board that service is the basis of your leadership?

4. Who were the best church leaders you have ever known? What were they like? How do their characteristics compare with the biblical criteria set forth for leaders in this chapter?

5. What continuing education does your board currently provide for its members? Would your board be open to discussing ways for members to cultivate a more vital relationship with God?

THE FAITH CHURCH
BOARD RETREAT HAD
DEEPLY AFFECTED
SALLY WALKER. SHE
HAD BEEN IN A SPIRI-
TUAL GROWTH GROUP
FOR SEVEN MONTHS
BEFORE BEING ELECT-
ED TO THE BOARD.
THUS IT SURPRISED
NO ONE AT THE NEXT
MONTHLY BOARD
MEETING WHEN SHE
SUGGESTED, "LET'S
MAKE A THOROUGH
STUDY OF THE RELA-
TIONSHIP JESUS HAD
WITH HIS DISCIPLES,
AS WELL AS LIFE IN
THE EARLY CHURCH."
THE BOARD QUICKLY
ADOPTED HER SUG-
GESTION.

CHAPTER 2

Becoming a Community of Christian Leaders

Leaders do not grow automatically. The church nurtures faith by providing for it, engaging in it, and holding leaders accountable.

This vision will come more clearly as we intentionally weave ourselves into a biblical community – an interdependent fellowship which glorifies God in Jesus Christ, in humility, through worship and service, by nurturing and being nurtured, and by exercising spiritual gifts.

WHAT THE BIBLE SAYS ABOUT BEING 'COMMUNITY'

1) Jesus and the twelve. Jesus' approach to community provides the foundation for becoming such an interdependent fellowship. His model reveals that *community begins with relationship.*

We read in Mark that, at the very outset of his ministry, Jesus "appointed twelve, whom he also named apostles, *to be with him…*" (Mk. 3:14, italics mine). In other words, Jesus selected the twelve for *fellowship.* As Norman Shawchuck and Roger Heuser have said, "He did not create this community for the others; he formed this community for himself. He felt the need to live out his ministry within the atmosphere of a small community, banded together, closer than brothers."[1]

What's more, Jesus maintained an "inner circle" including Peter, James, and John with whom he felt especially close. Only these disciples were present when he raised a twelve-year-old girl from death (Mk. 5:37), when he was transfigured on the mountain (Mk. 9:2), and during his agonizing last hours in the garden (Mk. 14:33). Thus at times Jesus leaned particularly on a smaller web of close friends for fellowship and support.

Jesus chose the disciples not only for fellowship but also for *ministry*. He hand-picked them to be the nucleus of his church, the new Israel. To complete Mark's description, Jesus "appointed the twelve...to be with him, and *to be sent out to proclaim the message...*" (Mk. 3:14, italics mine). Jesus sent out the twelve to expand his life-giving ministry. So, Jesus did not come to engage in isolated ministry but to build the foundation for the church; only in that way could he continue the inbreaking kingdom he had inaugurated.

Jesus actually developed this community of disciples into leaders through words, deeds, and example – a pattern we might follow today. First, Jesus taught his disciples. Through parables like the Good Samaritan (Lk. 10:25-37), teachings like the Sermon on the Mount (Matt. 5:1 - 7:28), and encounters like the one he had with the Rich Ruler (Lk. 18:18-30), Jesus helped his disciples glimpse the nature of the kingdom he was building.

Jesus also revealed love for God and others, with grace toward sinners and a simple wisdom that drew deeply from the lives of his hearers. He related his teachings to the work of their hands and common dimensions of their shared world.

Second, Jesus demonstrated faithful living through his deeds. For example, he embodied reconciliation in the presence of his disciples as he quietly received the homage of a sinful woman (Matt. 26:6-13). He rejected the seduction of empty flattery and stayed true to his convictions (Lk. 20:20-26). He was candid with his feelings, showing sorrow (Jn. 11:11-27), anger (Mk. 11:15-19), surprise (Matt. 8:10), and joy (Lk. 10:21-24). He forgave others (Lk. 7:48, 23:34).

Finally, Jesus modeled what he taught – harmonizing his words and deeds. He did not merely talk about service (Lk. 22:24-27), he lived it – kneeling to wash the disciples' dirty feet and charging them, "So if I, your Lord and Teacher, have washed your feet, you also ought to wash one another's feet" (Jn. 13:14).

Jesus also modeled certain means of grace. He "taught by example that six 'graces' were vital to his life and ministry: prayer, fasting, the Lord's Supper, the scriptures, spiritual conversation, and worship ..."[2] Though it's best to identify the Lord's Supper as a sacramental meal (Jesus did not institute the Lord's Supper until the end of his earthly life), *most of these means of grace will be directly incorporated into our understanding of a vital spirituality.* In all these ways Jesus nurtured faith, love, obedience, and mutuality in his followers.

2) The early Christians in Jerusalem. After the Holy Spirit was unleashed at Pentecost (Acts 2) and three thousand persons joined the Christian ranks, we read that they "devoted themselves to the apostles' teaching and fellowship, to the breaking of bread and the prayers" (Acts 2:42). In this amazing verse lies further help for us as we seek to build a community of disciples.

They devoted themselves to the apostles' teaching. This teaching focused on the person of Jesus Christ: his life, death, and resurrection (Acts 2:22-24). It concerned the kingdom of God resulting from Jesus' Messiahship and the new understanding of scripture he had given them. In addition, it keynoted the moral and ethical dimensions of his Messiahship. *Whenever we find a vital church today, we discover a church that is devoting itself to the apostles' teaching…in Sunday School classes, in Bible study groups, and in leadership training events.*

They devoted themselves to fellowship. As Jesus had done before them, the early Christians devoted themselves to fellowship, both with the apostles and the ever-increasing band of Christians. This fellowship, or *koinonia*, surpassed any they had known before – drawing them into communion with God through Jesus Christ and communion with others who called Jesus Lord. This communion enriched their lives so deeply that they shared all things, selling their possessions and distributing to any who had need (Acts 2:44-45). Amazingly, this fellowship erased the barriers between Jew and Gentile, slaves and free persons, men and women, and it created the basis for a new society. *Whenever we find a vital church today, we discover leaders who have deep communion with Jesus Christ and one another.*

They devoted themselves to the breaking of bread. The early Christians "broke bread at home" (Acts 2:46), sharing food with those who had none. They probably also engaged in the Lord's Supper. "The breaking of bread" seems to describe more than just the sharing of a common meal. Many scholars believe that the phrase depicts a ritual like the feeding of the five thousand and/or Jesus' action with his disciples at the Last Supper. In other words, they continued to celebrate sacramental fellowship with the risen Lord who had promised to be with them always. *The vitality of many churches is greatly strengthened by a deeper emphasis on fellowship with the risen Christ at his table.* For as the hymnist has said, "Here, O our

Lord, We see you face to face."[3]

They devoted themselves to the prayers. The early Christians prayed publicly in the temple, prayed in homes where they gathered for group and family prayers (Acts 12:12), and prayed personally. They prayed with rejoicing and they prayed in crises (Acts 12:5). Ardent prayer undergirded their worship and work; it added to their number day by day those who called Jesus Lord; it gave them courage when the world turned hostile; and it demonstrated a new depth of life. *Whenever we find a vital church today, we will discover people engaged in prayer…in their sanctuaries, in small groups, and in their homes.* Leaders of such churches know that prayer is the lifeblood of their fellowship.

Two other passages, Acts 4:32-37 and Acts 6:1-8, illumine the character of a vital church. In Acts 4 we see that "the whole group of those who believed were of one heart and soul, and no one claimed private ownership of any possessions, but everything they owned was held in common. With great power the apostles gave their testimony to the resurrection of the Lord Jesus, and great grace was upon them all." They embodied the tight linkage between *service* and *witness*. The apostles gave testimony to the resurrection of Jesus – and, without accident, "great grace was upon them all"; without accident, "there was not a needy person among them…" (Acts 4:34). Ministry is always a response to God's grace; service in the world results from hearing the Word proclaimed.

Note that the Christians in Jerusalem did not claim private ownership of anything, owning everything in common. Clearly their communal lifestyle was not practiced outside Jerusalem nor mandated for everyone in Jerusalem – only invited (Acts 5:4). Nor did it last. The crucial point: the early Christians were committed to sharing, to service, to taking care of the needy.

As we have noted, Acts 6:1-8 outlines the appointing of the seven to "wait tables" – with their promptly extending their mission to include vibrant witness and testimony (Acts 6:8-7:60, 8:26-40). And bearing in mind the example of Jesus – among the disciples "as one who serves," who waits on tables! – we may even question the apostles' suggestion to appoint the seven. They clearly attempted to separate service and witness, yet Jesus demonstrated that the two are intertwined. Indeed, those who are not willing to serve may lose credibility when they witness. *Whenever we find a vital church today, we find leaders who both serve and witness.*

By looking to the example of Jesus and the early Christians, we find many common threads that lend color and dimension to the ministry we must weave in our changing world. These threads outline a pattern for building Christian community and fostering spiritual growth:

- Fellowship
- Worship
- Prayer
- Scripture
- Sacramental meal
- Service
- Witness

BUILDING COMMUNITY ON NEW TESTAMENT FOUNDATIONS

Like the first century followers of Jesus, today's church faces an indifferent, sometimes hostile culture. We must learn from the example of Jesus and the early church because their proven model was formed in the crucible of cultural indifference and matured in the coliseums of cultural hostility.

Still, the patterns set forth in scripture do not serve as complete blueprints for officer leadership. More aptly, they resemble preliminary sketches which may be expanded into complete blueprints for a particular context.

While it seems unwise and impractical to replicate every ritual, practice, or idea embodied in the early church, we should take seriously the dynamics of their life together. For example, contrast the full prayer life of the early Christians with our faltering, spasmodic prayers. That failure alone can account for the fatigue and burnout plaguing many of today's leaders. In these days we must once again devote ourselves to "the prayers."

Consider how to adapt these ideas to a specific context. Focus on this question: How can we best mature into a community of leaders, using the scriptural foundations modeled by Jesus and the early Christians? Also, in the background, remember that by strengthening our personal commitment to fulfilling scriptural qualifications for leadership, we underline the value of corporate faith and the concept of "church as community."

Following the example of Jesus, we might meet in discipleship groups (either with lay leaders and members or with pastors and lay leaders) to emphasize fellowship, worship, prayer, scripture, service, witness, and, in some traditions, the sacramental meal. By learning from Jesus' words, deeds, and example, we may develop the humble, close bonds of fellowship that model the church at its best – growing as individuals and as the body of Christ.

Appendix C lists a possible pledge or "rule of life" for Christian leaders. The pledge fills the gap left by questions posed to church leaders at their installation. It shapes more specifically our intentions as church leaders to become the persons we were elected to be. The pledge builds on the graces we have studied and embodies elements of *knowing, being,* and *doing* the gospel. To grow as servant leaders, we should consider which parts of the pledge we are personally willing to observe – being careful not to choose more elements than we think we can keep. If we do, we will soon be overwhelmed with feelings of failure and may abandon the pledge altogether. However, we should identify some element from each of the three categories of knowing, being, and doing. In this way, we seek to mature by using the ancient means of grace and becoming accountable to one another for our practice.

QUESTIONS FOR FURTHER DISCUSSION

1. As you review the relationship Jesus had with his disciples, which of the six graces strike(s) you as most important?
2. How important is prayer in your board meetings?
3. What element stands out for you in reviewing the life of the early Christians in Jerusalem?
4. What immediate steps should your board take to become a community of leaders? What obstacles stand in the way?
5. As you evaluate "A Christian Leader's Pledge," which part is more difficult for you – knowing, being, or doing? What difference do you think it would make in your board and church if all leaders took the pledge seriously?

CHAPTER 3

Learning To Work as a Team in Ministry

"WE SPEND FAR TOO MUCH TIME AT OUR MEETINGS PUTTING OURSELVES UNDER A MICROSCOPE," FUMED A FRUSTRATED JOHN MARTIN AT A BOARD MEETING FOR FAITH CHURCH. A TEN MINUTE EVALUATION OF THE PRECEDING MEETING KINDLED JOHN'S ANGER. JOHN MARTIN'S OUTBURST ILLUSTRATES THE DIFFICULTY MANY CHURCH LEADERS HAVE WHEN THEY MOVE INTO NEW, MORE INTENTIONAL WAYS OF WORKING TOGETHER.

With relatively little pain we can acknowledge that we lead by serving, but it is another matter entirely to lead that way. After all, what do servant leaders look like in action?

We've realized already that servant leaders possess love, humility, and respect for people. But beyond this, to truly act as servant leaders we must follow the example of Jesus and the early Christians by learning how to work with one another *relationally*. That means listening to others as well as admitting and learning from our own mistakes.

Interestingly, while we pursue these qualities and practices because they are biblical, even top management theorists in the corporate world acknowledge that some of the most effective secular leaders follow these same principles.[1] Effective business leaders, findings show, often do not clutch at their authority but draw instead from the collective wisdom of all concerned. They collaborate and act supportively on behalf of those under their authority.

How much more important for *Christian* leaders to embrace these principles! When we do, we allow God's Spirit to blow where it will, bringing spiritual gifts, spiritual fruit, and prevailing wisdom to the whole community.

THE ART OF COLLABORATION

When we as Christian leaders collaborate, we reflect the spirit of the early church, which held all things in common (Acts 2:44). This is true because, by acting collaboratively, we choose to "hold in common" responsibility, power, and authority.

In short, we recognize and build upon our different roles within the body of Christ. To demonstrate: one's stomach might crave an orange which rests on a table across the room. The stomach will not be satisfied, however, until the brain communicates this to the rest of the body: the person's feet must carry her or him to the table; the hand must reach for and peel the orange, placing it in the mouth; the teeth and gums must contribute to prepare this wedge of fruit for the stomach…and so it goes. All parts of the body work together for the common good, contributing what they are uniquely created to contribute.

We best function together as a body when we maximize "two-way" communication. To build off the preceding scenario, the stomach communicates a need to the brain. The brain considers the need of the stomach, communicating back to the stomach the work required of the feet to cross the room and the hand to pick up and peel the orange, the consideration of others in the home if this is the final orange in the bowl, not to mention the scheduled time for supper and the feelings of the cook! The stomach responds to these issues, either yielding its will in homage to the cook, to other residents, or to the required work effort – or insisting that its hunger is most urgent. The brain responds by determining and acting on what seems best for the body, the cook, and any others in the home.

To develop a maximum flow of relevant information – and to ensure that the multiple issues facing the body of Christ are addressed – servant leaders conduct group meetings to make decisions. They invite all to participate openly; they freely share information with everyone.

The group habitually identifies problems and solves them. If the group cannot reach consensus, leaders make the decision, knowing that group members have shared all the relevant information. Servant leadership is characterized by confidence and trust in all matters between leaders and non-leaders. Morale and creativity generally blossom, as do productivity and joy.[2]

To be sure, knowing that we meet in the power of the Holy Spirit gives collaborative leadership in the church a unique dimension. We seek the Spirit's guidance and use the Spirit's gifts. This dimension of life is not consciously available to leaders in industrial and business leadership. When Christians meet, we pray for the Spirit as a body. And when the church stays close to Christ, who rules the church through Word and Spirit, it accesses a power that can produce astonishing results.

ACTING SUPPORTIVELY ON BEHALF OF OTHERS

Jesus supremely modeled supportive behavior. We see this trait in his tender response toward "sinners" and outcasts as well as in his lashing out against the powerful to support the demeaned. He demonstrated this supportive behavior when he paired and sent the seventy into every town and place where he intended to go (Lk. 10:1-12). Jesus appointed them, giving clear guidance ("Carry no purse, no bag, no sandals…" in v. 4) within an overarching context of freedom ("*Whatever* house you enter…" in v.5, italics mine). He sent them, trusting them to use keen judgment in following his instructions. And he affirmed them when they returned (Lk. 10:17-20), acknowledging their success and giving further gentle guidance (v.20).

Of course, we are not Jesus, but we can learn from Jesus' model in this scenario. He equipped those under his authority; gave them guidance without an exact script of "who, what, when, and where"; trusted them to act faithfully; listened to their reports; and affirmed the things they did correctly, while guiding gently when they were misfocused.

As flesh-and-blood humans we embody these characteristics and model servant leadership when we are friendly and open to others, when we listen well whether or not we agree with the speaker, when we encourage others to express their ideas fully and frankly, and when we display confidence and trust in others even when they do not agree with our positions. We demonstrate servant leadership when we seek solutions that are acceptable not only to us but also to those with whom we differ.[3]

As has been proven in the marketplace and in the church, the supportive leader provides more direction when the group proves ineffective in its work. At other times, supportive leaders merely supply emotional support to a group already working well on its task. Supportive leaders act responsibly in whatever way the situation requires.[4]

The supportive leader exercises power by sharing it with others, not by jealously guarding it. In short, the supportive leader functions "as one who serves" (Lk. 22:27).

LEARNING TO WORK TOGETHER AS THE BODY OF CHRIST

Servant leaders can be made and not merely born. We can train leaders. Significantly, the Holy Spirit equips us as we invite divine assistance. And, from a human perspective, role plays and other exercises (see Appendix B) help us identify and grow in the skills linked to servant leadership.

God gives us the desire and ability to be servant leaders. We begin by examining six qualities identified by management theorist Rensis Likert for effective leadership – and observing their important relationship to biblical, servant leadership.

1. Supportiveness. The most effective leaders in business and industry reflect supportive behavior. So, it seems, do the most effective church leaders. In *Let My People Go*, Alvin Lindgren and Norman Shawchuck say that "When members perceive that the leader has a genuine appreciation of their personal worth and of their importance, as well as patient concern for their welfare, a sense of trust emerges. This opens communication channels, increases their willingness to risk new ventures, and {fosters} a spirit of cooperation."[5]

Yet the members must perceive that their leaders are supportive; it's not enough for *leaders* to consider their behavior supportive. Only now has the church begun to recognize the crucial role of supportive behavior in all dimensions of leadership. The way leaders listen to those with whom they work, respond to their questions, take an interest in their careers and community activities, listen to their problems, and relate to them generally will be perceived as either supportive or unsupportive.

2. Openness and receptivity. One of the most difficult tasks a leader faces is maintaining an open and receptive posture when people bubble over with ideas or when they hold different views. Leaders may wince when an enthusiastic member proposes using "off-brand" Sunday school literature that is theologically shallow. Even so, is it not important to learn how to affirm the person, express an interest in the idea, and look for any merit in what has been proposed?

At the same time, leaders must retain their own integrity. To balance these tensions and to search for a way to resolve them proves challenging. But *ideas will stop flowing* unless leaders create an accepting climate for them – and that would be tragic since the church ideally is committed to using the gifts, talents, and ideas of all members. Ministry can be exciting when leaders stay open and receptive to their members.

3. Team building. A team-building leader tries to harmonize and use all the talents and gifts of fellow members, believing the team will achieve higher productivity and greater satisfaction. Servant leaders use their own gifts as well as the gifts of all members of the body of Christ, knowing that "to each is given the manifestation of the Spirit for the common good" (1 Cor. 12:7).

Moreover, supportive leaders believe a team of people can be more effective than one person in working on problems. Thus they seek to develop their skills in drawing forth solutions from the group. They also know that those who take part in making decisions will be more enthusiastic in carrying them out. As Christian leaders, we will do well to follow the example of Paul who refused to succumb to a divisive "party spirit" that erupted among the Corinthian Christians (1 Cor. 3:5). Paul instead saw himself as part of a team of fellow workers and, indeed, described team members as *servants*.

Moreover, wise leaders will train fellow-workers in the principles of good team relationships. They will show how the church consists of a series of interlocking teams – just as a cardiovascular system, digestive system, and reproductive system all work in harmony within one human body.

4. Helping members with their work. Nothing can destroy a leader's effectiveness more quickly than aloofness, which communicates disinterest or superiority. Leaders must respond to members who ask for help. For example, what will the Church School Superintendent do when a teacher asks her to recommend resources for teaching next Sunday's lesson? This request is valid, but a response requires time and interest. Leaders who communicate that they are approachable, available, and eager to serve find volunteers much more willing to work with them. Long ago Paul gave the biblical basis for this skill when he said, "Bear one another's burdens, and in this way you will fulfill the law of Christ" (Gal. 6:2). Only at the end of the passage did he say, "For all must carry their own loads" (Gal. 6:5).

Specifically, how do leaders help others with their work and hence bear their burdens? By

- understanding and clarifying their needs
- readily sharing useful information
- identifying resources
- following up to express interest in how things are going.

5. Expecting excellence from others. Supportive leaders maintain high performance expectations for themselves and for those with whom they work. They believe people want to be identified with high quality performance and "that when they are engaged in work they believe to be important, they will want to give it their best."[6] This means supportive leaders do not readily tolerate mediocrity in the work of others – an astounding concept if applied to the church! Supportive leaders believe that valuing quality translates into valuing persons.

Paul demonstrated the same principle when he wrote to the Corinthians, "According to the grace of God given to me, like a skilled builder, I laid a foundation, and someone else is building on it. Each builder must choose with care how to build on it" (1 Cor. 3:10,11).

But how many church leaders really expect excellence from their members? More often than not they expect mediocrity because "if you put many demands on volunteers, they may quit!" But expecting mediocrity becomes a self-fulfilling prophecy. On the other hand, when leaders who model excellence expect it, members are more likely to perform well. What leaders expect, they usually get!

6. Group methods of decision making. Many denominations, including my own, rely on *Robert's Rules of Order* or other formal procedures to make decisions. But formal decision-making procedures can intimidate people, lock them into adversarial positions, create hurt feelings, and lead to unwise decisions. Even so, such procedures may be particularly necessary in large group settings. The sheer size of a group may render group discussion all but impossible.

In smaller groups, however, more informal decision-making methods work better. Whenever appropriate and permitted by one's church, leaders should help build a warm, accepting climate in which people can express their ideas freely, learn from one another, and attempt to reach decisions by consensus as they are guided by the Holy Spirit. How much better it is to train people to listen carefully to one another, build on their ideas, and strive for win-win solutions when possible!

Good servant-leaders employ these relational and task skills to help them as they work together and with church members in mission and ministry. Remember three things: 1) the spiritual base of leadership is fundamental – leaders grow in servanthood which requires love, humility, and respect; 2) collaboration, empowered by the Holy Spirit, is essential in reaching decisions; and

3) supportive leadership skills must be practiced. *Most church leaders are thrown into decision-making situations but are given no training in how to make those decisions.*

The schema that follows shows how leaders and members can work together in ministry for the common good.[7]

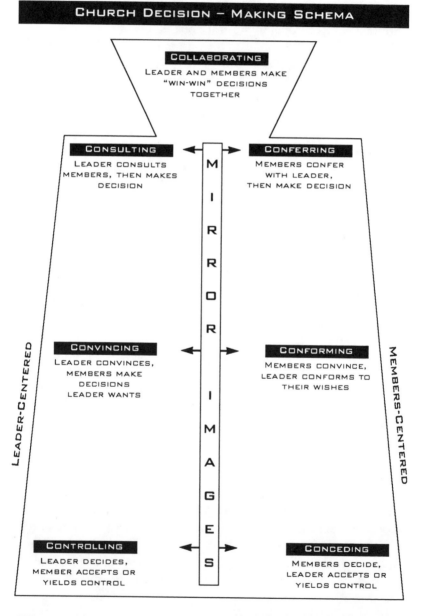

CHURCH DECISION – MAKING SCHEMA

COLLABORATING
LEADER AND MEMBERS MAKE
"WIN-WIN" DECISIONS
TOGETHER

CONSULTING
LEADER CONSULTS
MEMBERS, THEN MAKES
DECISION

CONFERRING
MEMBERS CONFER
WITH LEADER,
THEN MAKE DECISION

MIRROR IMAGES

CONVINCING
LEADER CONVINCES,
MEMBERS MAKE
DECISIONS
LEADER WANTS

CONFORMING
MEMBERS CONVINCE,
LEADER CONFORMS TO
THEIR WISHES

CONTROLLING
LEADER DECIDES,
MEMBER ACCEPTS OR
YIELDS CONTROL

CONCEDING
MEMBERS DECIDE,
LEADER ACCEPTS OR
YIELDS CONTROL

LEADER-CENTERED

MEMBERS-CENTERED

In working with churches I have not only observed a movement from leader-centered behavior to mutual decision-making, but also a progression of member-centered behavior from conferring to conceding. When church members take the lead in making decisions, as they often do in small churches, the minister is involved in varying degrees. However, in some situations ministers virtually concede all responsibility to church boards and members. Because these member-centered decision-making patterns are fairly common in the church, I added these three dimensions, which are really mirror images of the leader-centered styles on the other side of the schema.

In further examining the schema, we do well to think about how our church board and committees characteristically make decisions. Note that each style has a positive and a negative quality.

In the *controlling* style, for example, it's positive when a leader makes a decision in a crisis. Who has time to call a board meeting when the church is on fire? But controlling is a negative style when leaders deny others ownership, neglect their creativity, and squeeze them out of the decision-making process.

The *convincing* style is positive when a leader uses personal expertise and teaches, persuades, and convinces, particularly when members have a gap in their knowledge. But it's negative when a leader connives with only a few members in the process, leaves out the rest, and sets up a competitive situation among them.

A *consulting* style is positive when the leader asks members for their opinions and then incorporates these into decision making. It's negative, however, when the leader asks their opinions only as a ploy, with no intention to be influenced by what they say.

The favored *collaborating* style is positive when leader and members can reach a mutual decision that leads them to say, "We did it together!" Yet it may be negative if leader and members compromise too quickly around the lowest common denominator for the sake of unity.

In the *conferring* style, the mirror image of consulting, the members act positively by including the leader in decisions and allowing themselves to be influenced by the leader's opinions. But this style is negative if they do this only as a polite gesture to make the leader think his or her opinion really matters.

In the *conforming* style members persuade and convince the leader that they know what is best. That's positive as long as they have expertise that the leader does not have. Yet this approach can also be negative when they are more interested in convincing the leader than in being influenced by the leader.

In the *conceding* style members simply make the decision and expect the leader to go along. This style can be positive if the leader willingly abdicates control because he or she knows that the members, because of their expertise and history, know what is best. It's negative, on the other hand, when the members ignore the leader and expect him or her to concede to their wishes and demands.

All these observations are designed to give insight into how we lead and how we *might* lead, so we can compare our styles with the biblical record. Ideally, from there, we will grow toward a healthy biblical model.

As we face cultural changes of extraordinary dimensions, Christian leaders must learn to meet cultural demands with a biblical grasp of the unique call of leadership. Never before have church leaders needed to work together more than they do now.

QUESTIONS FOR FURTHER DISCUSSION

1. WHAT SERVANT LEADERS HAVE YOU KNOWN IN YOUR CHURCH EXPERIENCE? WHAT CHARACTERISTICS DID THEY EMBODY? WHAT WAS THE EFFECT OF THEIR LEADERSHIP?

2. WHAT IS MOST DIFFICULT FOR YOU PERSONALLY AS YOU THINK ABOUT BECOMING A SERVANT LEADER? MIGHT CONTEMPORARY WOMEN HAVE PARTICULAR PROBLEMS WITH SERVANT LEADERSHIP?

3. HOW ARE DECISIONS USUALLY MADE IN YOUR LEADERSHIP MEETINGS? TO WHAT EXTENT DO YOU COLLABORATE BY SEEKING THE INPUT OF ALL? IS INFORMATION FREELY SHARED AMONG ALL LEADERS WHEN YOU MAKE DECISIONS?

4. HAVE YOUR LEADERS RECEIVED ANY TRAINING IN THE PRINCIPLES OF COLLABORATION? WHAT DIFFERENCE WOULD IT MAKE IN THE WORK OF YOUR COMMITTEES IF THEY WERE TRAINED TO SHARE MINISTRY MORE FULLY?

5. WHAT STEPS SHOULD YOUR BOARD TAKE NOW TO IMPROVE HOW IT MAKES DECISIONS AND SHARES MINISTRY?

CHAPTER 4

Meeting the Challenges of a New Day

Anyone who watches the evening news, or reads the staggering reports of societal violence, or considers statistics about the unforeseen decay of the family likely agrees that our culture stands at a crossroads. Turmoil and change lurk everywhere. Indeed, many would describe our situation as a crisis.

This crisis, this turmoil and change, has seeped through the pages of the culture at large and into the traditional church in North America. While it may be hidden from all but the most observant – especially when worship services proceed as usual, children and adults attend Sunday school as before, boards still meet to govern and plan, and churches provide fellowship and service opportunities – *change has come and is coming.* Never mind that on the surface it appears as though nothing has changed.

FAITH CHURCH BOARD MEMBER CYNTHIA HERERA HAD JUST RETURNED FROM A DENOMINATIONAL CONFERENCE ON FAMILY LIFE. OVERWHELMED BY WHAT SHE HAD HEARD ABOUT THE PROBLEMS FACING FAMILIES, SHE BLURTED OUT IN A BOARD MEETING ONE NIGHT, "WE ARE FACING A CRISIS IN EVERY DIRECTION WE LOOK, AND HERE WE SIT ARGUING ABOUT WHICH LAWN SERVICE TO USE. WHY DO WE ACT AS THOUGH NOTHING IS HAPPENING? PARADIGMS ARE SHIFTING ALL AROUND US, EVEN AS WE SPEAK."

This tumultuous change results from what theologians and sociologists call a "paradigm shift." And if we are to be effective as Christian leaders in a new day, we will do well to understand the cause and effect of the paradigm shift facing the church.

WHAT IS A 'PARADIGM SHIFT'?

A paradigm is an example, a pattern – a small scale model of a large concept that is difficult to understand. Embedded deep in all paradigms lie basic assumptions, rules, and regulations about how we see and do things – as well as how we justify what we see and do.

Any major shift in scientific theory, business practice, or theology may be described as a paradigm shift. For example, when Polish astronomer Nicolaus Copernicus suggested in the 16th century that the earth and other planets orbit around the sun, he broke from the earlier Ptolemaic model which suggested the earth was the center of the universe. Copernicus's model was branded as outlandish, his revolutionary ideas, heretical. Even *considering* that the earth was not the center of the universe rattled ancient understandings about life, the preeminence of humanity, and even God.

In other words, the older Ptolemaic theory undergirded ancient beliefs about life, humanity, and God, and likewise these ancient beliefs undergirded scientific understandings. No one foresaw that a new perspective would force people everywhere to rethink their previous justifications. Yet when other scientists scrutinized the new concept and conducted their own experiments, the scientific community reached consensus that Copernicus was right. And other thoughts and beliefs were revised in kind.

In the realm of business, the most striking paradigm shift may have occurred in Switzerland in the late 1960s. At that time the paradigm or model for watchmaking was the well-engineered Swiss motion timepiece and, as late as 1968, Swiss watchmakers commanded 65 percent of the world watch market. Their technique was the industry standard. Then a Swiss research group developed the quartz movement watch. Swiss watchmakers didn't take the new development seriously, though, because it was so different from the traditional technique they had perfected. Only ten years later the Swiss controlled less than 10 percent of the world watch market! A paradigm shift was occurring but they did not see it. They "got stuck in history and history left them behind."[1]

Another societal paradigm shift of major proportions has been launched in recent decades with the emerging role of women. More than 46 percent of today's work force is comprised of women, and this has far-reaching implications for business, family, and the church.

The Church's Paradigm

The Christian Church has existed under two paradigms in its two thousand year history. Loren Mead describes the first one as the Apostolic Paradigm. In this model Jesus sent forth people into an often hostile world to convert it and care for it. At the heart of the early church was a local community, a congregation called out of the world. It was, as Mead describes it, "an intimate community, whose being demanded that it serve and care for a world hostile to itself..."[2]

This Apostolic Paradigm characterized the church from its birth until 313 A.D., when Emperor Constantine converted to Christianity and established the faith as the official religion of the Roman Empire. Ten years later Constantine defeated Licinius, ruler of the East, and became sole ruler of the empire. "The church, for all practical purposes, had now become the church of the state."[3]

Thus Constantine inaugurated what has been named the Constantinian Church, or what Mead calls the Christendom Paradigm – what others call the Establishment Church Paradigm. Under this model, Christianity no longer operated in a hostile environment; it became the official religion of all Western empires. Every citizen of the empire was automatically a member of the church – and since all neighbors were Christian also, no one needed to witness to the mighty acts of God in Jesus Christ. Thus, the church was no longer in the missionary posture that had characterized the Apostolic Paradigm. The environment was friendly, not hostile.

Seventeen centuries later, however, the North American offspring of the Roman Empire – the United States and Canada – have officially separated church and state. Still, until recently, a very favorable *informal* relationship existed. Now even that relationship is rapidly dissolving. Blue laws, which once undergirded the Christian Sabbath as a day of rest for businesses or from liquor sales, are now virtually extinct; prayer in public schools has been deemed unconstitutional. Immigrants from various countries, practicing myriad religions, now populate these two nations long-dominated by European descendants, and they demand equal attention and respect. In short, the Christian faith no longer enjoys a "most favored religion" status in North America.

The paradigm is changing, and, like the Swiss watchmakers of the last generation, we must observe and adapt to the change. But this shifting Christendom Paradigm has left us confused. The state and many of its citizens look at the church with new eyes, frequently with indifference, occasionally with disdain, sometimes with outright hostility.

Should the church face the breakdown of the Christendom

Paradigm by fighting to maintain an informal relationship with the state, along with its accompanying blessings? Or should we consider our new situation as a challenge to become a missionary church once again? Stanley Hauerwas and William Willimon celebrate this moment as an opportunity "for American Christians to be faithful in a way that makes being a Christian an exciting adventure."[4]

THE BREAKDOWN OF THE CHURCH

This paradigm shift relates specifically to the context of ministry and the relationship between the church and culture, yet we find that more than paradigms are changing. Indeed, the core life of the church itself is threatened. Declining membership, shrinking budgets, organizational downsizing, and church closings mark the decline.

At the root of these systemic problems lies one conspicuous truth: for all our church busy-ness, we are losing contact with the faith and we are missing a new generation of persons.
To demonstrate, as a church we are largely biblically illiterate, losing contact with the Bible stories and events that shape our identity. Moreover, even those of us in leadership tend to blur the significance of the person and work of Jesus Christ.

I once attended a meeting of newly elected church officers who had completed extensive training in preparation for examination. The officers were asked to comment on their Christian experience, and one by one they began to share. One spoke of growing up in another denomination in a different part of the country. Another mentioned attending church as a child, drifting away in young adulthood, and then returning when their first child was born. On and on the sharing continued, as I observed in astonishment. *Not one person mentioned anything about being related to Jesus Christ as Savior and Lord!*

Was the relationship so obvious to them as not to require mention? No, I believe it was because it did not occur to them – perhaps because it may not have been a vital part of their core faith. Yet, if we maintain only a vague "We go to church because it's important" notion, the church is clearly losing contact with the faith that has nourished it. We are part of this unique community of persons precisely because Jesus is Savior and Lord, and here we intentionally seek to worship and know him better.

We also find other clues that the church is losing its moorings. Parents, for example, no longer share the faith with their children as in times past. A survey conducted by the Presbyterian Church (U.S.A.) revealed that 58 percent of Presbyterian adolescents have never spoken with their fathers about faith, and 63 percent have never had family worship. Is it any wonder John Westerhoff wrote a book entitled, *Will Our Children Have Faith?*

The obstinacy of many church governing boards and congregations provides a final indicator among numerous possible clues. When we as church leaders desperately struggle to maintain the status quo and balk at the simplest changes, we demonstrate that today's church has lost contact with the One who said, "See, I am making all things new" (Rev. 21:5). We show ourselves more protective of the way things have been than interested in any new work of God's Spirit. We further give evidence of our insensitivity to those outside the church.

The Breakdown of Society

Rightly we wonder whether Western society is falling apart. Is poet William Butler Yeats right when he says, "Things fall apart the centre cannot hold....The best lack all conviction, while the worst Are full of passionate intensity?"[5] Several emerging phenomena in the United States portend deep trouble ahead.

In the aftermath of the 1992 Los Angeles riots, experts asked, "What were the motives of the rioters? What perceptions did they have?" According to their answers, the rioters felt separated and disconnected from the dominant group. In short, they were afflicted with the deadly disease of *alienation*. When persons feel alienated, they often lash out at whatever they think oppresses them. Today's exploding national crime offers dramatic testimony to the alienation and sense of meaninglessness plaguing numerous citizens.

On a smaller scale, many of us feel increasingly alienated in our own country. More and more we say we are confused by the changing demographics of the nation we once knew. When and why the flood of immigrants? What is happening to the Euro-American base to which many of us belong? Can we accept the startling prediction that in the not-too-distant future various ethnic groups will outnumber Euro-Americans? In face of such massive societal change, some people have been unable or unwilling to see the present moment as an opportunity for America to become a universal nation composed of people from diverse cultures and religions.

Add to the symptom of alienation yet another symptom: *the*

rapidly changing family. Between 1970 and 1990, for example, the proportion of children living with a parent who had never been married quadrupled. Also, the proportion of children in single-parent families mushroomed until in 1993 more than 16 million U. S. children lived with only one parent.

Why the startling increase in single-parenthood? It cannot be accounted for solely by teen pregnancies in low income families or by the fact that some affluent, well-educated women choose to become single parents. Rather, divorce is now the leading cause of single-parenthood in all industrial countries where it is legal. And single-parent homes, as many observers have pointed out, often take a toll on the children, their parents, and society.

Of course, many beleaguered single parents are struggling bravely to hold their families together and teach them strong values. They sometimes say, however, that they feel like salmon swimming upstream, overwhelmed with the task of being both father and mother in a fragmented culture.

Other alarming statistics abound. We could easily focus on drugs, spousal and child abuse, the growing problem of homelessness, the lack of adequate health care among millions of low income Americans, and the proliferation of guns, with children shooting children. Yet consider the *loss of character* that besieges us from all sides.

Such loss of character can be easily seen in many of the following facets of our life today:
• irresponsible fathers who leave pregnant women to fend for themselves without offering their support;
• unrestrained individualists who want to live and die unto themselves, unmoved by the cries of others to join them in working for the common good;
• rampant greed that drives many of us to measure everything by how much money we can make and how many possessions we can acquire;
• insatiable lust that targets people as sex objects and thrives on ever increasing stimulation and desire;
• a burning quest for more and more technological knowledge without the concurring power of love.

Add the loss of character, then, to the sense of alienation and the disintegration of the family as major evidences of social breakdown.

When we consider the dissolution of the Christendom Paradigm along with the breakdown of the church and the breakdown of society, we recognize the need for the immediate attention of all disciples of Jesus Christ. How much more important, then, becomes the call for attention and action from Christian leaders. As such, we may choose to dismiss the crisis as a momentary blip on the radar screen of humankind – in the same way Swiss watchmakers dismissed the new-fangled quartz movement technology that led to their demise. Or we may choose to face the crisis honestly and live into it.

The crisis can be, as the word itself means, a "turning point." This may occur if we, as leaders:

- help the church to shift its focus from maintaining a favored status to being true to the gospel;
- show the church how to anchor itself more fully to Jesus Christ;
- boldly proclaim and live the gospel of Jesus Christ and help others do the same;
- embrace the unique calling to be a community belonging to Jesus Christ;
- lead the congregation into renewed commitment to the reconciling Christ who can overcome the alienation of the world;
- encourage the church to enable torn persons, destabilized by changing mores, to be strengthened in the inner person by God's Spirit;
- demonstrate the surpassing value of being faithful to Christ rather than successful in the world's eyes;
- help the church stand firmly against dehumanizing structures that threaten to undo the very fabric of society.

We can make this a positive turning point, in short, if we help the church decide to be the church and to do the work of the church!

I am convinced the church cannot negotiate all these turning points without faithful and effective leadership – particularly from lay leaders. While obviously members must play a vital role in responding to the crisis, they are not likely to do so without dynamic leadership. Leaders always exert powerful influence upon those with whom they work, for followers tend to replicate the behavior of their leaders.

As leaders, we can learn from the costly indifference of Swiss watchmakers. We can help pilot the church in a new direction under the leadership of the Holy Spirit. We play a pivotal role in helping the church to navigate the choppy waters of change. By reading the storm signals in culture and placing a firm hand on the mast of faith, we can and must lead the church into a dynamic new day.

QUESTIONS FOR FURTHER DISCUSSION

1. What evidence do you see in your church and community of the crisis facing modern society?

2. Has the Christendom or Establishment Church Paradigm given way to a new paradigm where you live? Does the church enjoy a privileged status in your community? What reasons do you give to support your answer?

3. When you examine your church life, what evidence do you see for the breakdown of the church? Does your church board strongly resist change?

4. What instances, if any, of alienation and "loss of character" do you see in your community?

5. Why is leadership so important in turning the present crisis into an opportunity? What first steps can your leaders take to meet the present crisis?

Our Shared Leadership Task

Whatever our denomination, leadership structure, or church polity, I am convinced we share a common call: *Christian leaders guide the church as a people called by God to be a sign, a foretaste, and an instrument of the kingdom of God.*[1]

All our efforts to emulate the business world or civic organizations in making decisions, raising money, or conducting business trace their roots to a common misunderstanding. And while we can never extricate ourselves completely from the culture (nor perhaps should we), the church is not called to be like any other organization. While other groups may serve humanity or accomplish noble ends, only the church is called to be a sign, a foretaste, and an instrument of the kingdom of God.

To accomplish this requires that we become a community of discernment. As church leaders, we strive to ensure that the church becomes, participates in, witnesses to, demonstrates, and serves the reign of God. Those desired end-results should shape every mission statement we design, every activity we consider, every service we conduct, every budget we raise, every visit we make, every building we build, every leader we train.

As Christian leaders facing the challenges of a new day, we must refrain from the easy temptation to import culture into the church. Instead, we must enable the church *to be the church* and to influence the culture. What a reversal! Church leaders should raise this issue; it provides the starting blocks for living in tomorrow's unchurched culture. We must systematically and routinely ask about everything we do: *Does our action/ plan/ decision/ service reflect life in the kingdom of God?*

To ensure that the identity and distinctive mission of the church survives, we need to look toward those who are most steeped in the memory of the Christ event for guidance.[2] Or, to state it more dynamically, Christ still rules the church by Word and Spirit. That means the church must draw upon the wisdom of its theologically trained persons – both ministers and church leaders who have been equipped for their roles. Such leaders need to reflect theologically on current issues out of their biblical studies, and then they should help the church make decisions in light of the gospel story. Our most helpful role as leaders is to make proposals that arise from a Christian perspective.

Bearing in mind that other members may be deeply committed Christians who also make proposals from a Christian perspective, leaders must steer a middle course between deciding what a group should do and merely providing information for a group to make a decision. Our proposals should elicit reflection and discussion, leaving the decision making to the appropriate church bodies.[3] As we seek to guide the church to be a people called by God to be a sign, a foretaste, and an instrument of the kingdom of God, we begin by understanding the nature of the Christian church itself. Our understanding of leadership should grow out of a biblical conception of the church.

THE CHURCH AS THE PEOPLE OF GOD

Of the 96 rich metaphors of the church in the New Testament,[4] two seem particularly useful for our leadership focus: "the people of God" and "body of Christ" (which we will consider in Chapter 7).

"The community of faith in the Bible," Paul Hanson has said, "is the people called. It is the people called forth from diverse sorts of bondage to freedom, called to a sense of identity founded on the common bond with the God of righteousness and compassion, and called to the twin vocations of worship and participation in the creative, redemptive purpose that unifies all history and is directed to the restoration of the whole creation within a universal order of shalom."[5] And we belong to the church, a people called by God!

"A people called" is deeply rooted in the Old Testament in the call of Abraham. His call, though it came to him personally, was not an individual call and pilgrimage, but the call and pilgrimage of a particular people, a people who would be a blessing for all humankind. Through Abraham, God promised land to the landless, a seed, and a blessing for others. The church today stands as heir to those promises God made to Abraham. With Abraham and Sarah, and with the church down through the ages, we still listen for God's call, try to understand it, and seek to obey it faithfully. Note several significant aspects of the "people of God" image. First, as Paul Minear makes clear, people in general do not exist; only particular peoples exist. "Every person belongs to a particular people, just as he belongs to a particular tongue or nation or tribe; and this people is not reducible to the mathematical aggregate of its members. The people defines the person..."[6] As the church, we belong to the people *of God*. Our belonging defines who we are.

This understanding avoids elitism because it is not an arrogant claim to power and absolute virtue for itself. The accent in the Bible, as Minear puts it, is on God, and on God's faithful action in creating a people to carry out God's purpose. They were a people only because God called them, God claimed them, God sustained them, God saved them, and God judged them.[7] And we are God's own people, not to proclaim our greatness but the greatness of God.

God's call of us to be God's people entails enormous responsibility. "The purpose of the call," notes Walter Brueggemann, "is to fashion an alternative community in creation gone awry, to embody in human history the power of the blessing. It is the hope of God that in this new family all human history can be brought to the unity and harmony intended by the one who calls."[8]

That purpose sets forth the parameters for our work as leaders...to fashion an alternative community...to bring all people to the unity and harmony intended by God. We move inward to fashion a community; we move outward to bring all people to the shalom God intends for humanity.

So God calls us to fulfill God's purposes, not our own – an affront to many who think the church exists to meet our needs. The church does meet our needs but only when we worship and glorify God and seek to carry out God's purposes in the world. And God wants the church to reflect the kingdom of God.

THE CHURCH AND THE KINGDOM OF GOD

The church as a sign of the kingdom. The church represents the rule of God in its life; it points to the life, death, and resurrection of Jesus Christ,[9] to the power and love of God, not self-righteously to itself. As the Apostle Peter wrote to the exiles of the Dispersion: "But you are a chosen race, a royal priesthood, a holy nation,

God's own people, in order that you may proclaim the mighty acts of him who called you out of darkness into his marvelous light" (1 Pet. 2:9). So the church proclaims God's mighty acts to show that God is working in the here and now of history, in the history of our specific congregations as their lives unfold day by day.

Thus the church must participate in and bear witness to the rule of God in history, accomplishing this through its *worship* and *ministry*. Whenever we see a church gathered in worship to read, proclaim, and hear the Word faithfully; engaged in fervent prayer; and observing the sacraments with integrity, that church acts as a sign of God's reign.

The church also bears witness to the reign of God in its ministry. Whenever we see a church feeding the hungry, housing the homeless, or caring for the sick; working on behalf of the oppressed, for reconciliation in communities torn apart by drug-related crime, or for more effective D.U.I. laws; or caring for God's earth by preaching holistic stewardship or recycling precious resources or protecting the environment – that church acts as a sign of God's reign.

The church as a foretaste of the kingdom. A foretaste is a small sample in the present of something that will be enjoyed fully in the future. And the church, in its worship and ministry, affords such a taste – sometimes a rich taste indeed! – of the life we will know when the kingdom comes fully. In that day we who belong to the kingdom will taste completely what we have partly experienced here. The fellowship, joy, acceptance, and grace which have often blessed us in the church will pale in comparison to the fellowship, joy, acceptance, and grace we will know in that hour. In the meantime, however, we taste the new reality of life in the kingdom that Jesus gives us in the church.

Whenever members share in worship, fellowship, prayer, nurture, and service, they demonstrate vividly and concretely the life all people need and want.

The church must serve as a "contrast society" in order to provide a foretaste of the kingdom of God. Life in the kingdom must not mirror life in the world, which is marked so often by alienation, moral confusion, rampant individualism, and loss of soul. On the contrary, kingdom life displays reconciliation, moral discernment, communal richness, and integrity of heart. Unless the church exhibits such qualities in its worship and ministry, the world will continue to be indifferent, even hostile, to our presence.

But whenever the church acts in a manner that demonstrates the reality of the gospel, the world will notice – and believe. In the interim, we can know that if reconciliation does not happen *to* us, it will not happen *through* us.

As church leaders, we set up ministries, establish programs, and strengthen family life to demonstrate in flesh-and-blood fashion that our life is hidden with Christ in God. To determine whether the quality of church life serves as a foretaste of the kingdom of God, we must ask whether our life together truly reflects life in the kingdom.

To be a foretaste, we must intentionally build Christian community – working in humility together, drawing from the spiritual gifts of all, and discerning together the unique and new leadership of the Holy Spirit. To be a foretaste of the kingdom of God, the church must be the church in word and deed – which requires extraordinary leaders. Not leaders who are extraordinarily gifted – only leaders who are extraordinarily open to the Holy Spirit and who earnestly pray for God's kingdom to come here on earth as it is in heaven.

The church as an instrument of the kingdom. To discern what it means for the church to be an instrument, we must return to the wisdom of Jesus who summoned us to the task. Before an astonished congregation at the synagogue in his home town, Jesus unrolled the scroll from the prophet Isaiah and read words that have stamped themselves indelibly upon the church ever since: "The Spirit of the Lord is upon me, because he has anointed me to bring good news to the poor. He has sent me to proclaim release to the captives and recovery of sight to the blind, to let the oppressed go free, to proclaim the year of the Lord's favor. And he rolled up the scroll, gave it back to the attendant, and sat down" (Lk. 4:18-20).

In Jesus' words we have a broad outline of the instrumental work of the church. The One who was called to bring good news to the poor and recovery of sight to the blind sent his disciples to do the same. And he still sends the church today.

Despite the attempts of some to separate the church permanently from the world, the gospel bids us to join God in what God is doing in the world. While we may become an alternative community, we do not insulate ourselves from the world but prepare ourselves to serve the world better. For we know God cares about poverty, injustice, oppression, and sickness.

So must we, because through Jesus Christ, God has cared for us and set us free from every chain that would bind us. When we taste that freedom, then "through love we become slaves to one another" (Gal. 5:13). We seek to build up the church, but we move out into the world to proclaim the good news to all creation.

To be an instrument of the kingdom, therefore, the church "participates in the actualization of the coming reign of God in the world, proclaiming God's liberating power in word and deed, presenting an alternative identity and vision, seeking freedom, equality, and justice, pursuing peace and unity for all creation."[10] Not exactly a challenge for the lazy or fainthearted!

The focus of our work must shift from what we do in the church to what we do in the world. To be sure, our worship, nurture, pastoral care, and Bible studies will continue to equip us for what we do in the world. As Jesus both worshiped in the synagogue and moved out among the people, we must worship as a body and then move beyond our four walls into the world where people are hurting and dying. Indeed the present crisis begs for the church to become a missionary church once again.

Presently the world may shrug at the church's beliefs or ethical stances – and the world and the church probably stand on entirely different platforms. To influence the world for the sake of the kingdom may require us to learn the language of the marketplace and then examine it in light of the gospel. We cannot rely on old church cliches and patterns. And we dare not abandon the public arena to those who have no knowledge of Jesus, who cares for the poor and homeless, the captives and the oppressed, and who calls us to do likewise.

To guide the church to be a sign, a foretaste, and an instrument of the kingdom of God proves a formidable, but not impossible, task for church leaders. As we move out, we are empowered by the Holy Spirit – the same Spirit who rushed upon the world at Pentecost, who emboldened Peter to speak to thousands in Jerusalem, who guided the apostles and elders in the Jerusalem council meeting, and who equips us to be the church in our day and time.

Questions for Further Discussion

1. If you had to reduce the task of leaders to one sentence, what would it be?

2. What difference do you think it would make if your church considered itself "a people called"? What are the strengths and difficulties of this metaphor? What evidence do you find that you already so regard yourselves?

3. What difference might it make within your leadership and your church if you judged all proposals by whether or not they are a sign, or foretaste, or instrument of the kingdom of God?

4. What clues indicate that your church is now a sign of the kingdom of God? a foretaste? an instrument? What steps might you take to move in that direction?

5. Does your church resist the concept of being an instrument of God in all of life? Do you agree that the church should respond to issues of poverty, oppression, and injustice? If so, how?

THE FAITH CHURCH BOARD WAS INVOLVED IN A HEATED DISCUSSION OVER A PROPOSED "FAITH AND WORK" CONFERENCE. MANY AGREED WITH LEON HILL WHEN HE VEHEMENTLY DECLARED, "OUR BUDGET IS DOWN, THE SUNDAY SCHOOL NEEDS MORE TEACHERS, OUR MEMBERSHIP GROWTH IS LAGGING, AND WE ARE TALKING ABOUT THE RELATIONSHIP BETWEEN OUR FAITH AND OUR JOBS. THAT'S NOT WHERE WE OUGHT TO PUT OUR ENERGY. LEAVE THE WORKPLACE TO ADDRESS ITS OWN CONCERNS."

CHAPTER 6

Sharing the Vision with Church Members

Stirred by the present crisis and fueled by the Holy Spirit, today's church leaders must intentionally and sensitively guide the church as a people called by God. To accomplish this, we are challenged to resist the age-old temptation to center the focus of members on the assistance ministers need within the church – choosing, rather, to guide the church to reflect the reign of God in the world.

As we move into the 21st century, is it not important to concentrate on what the whole people of God can do together to help the church become what God wants it to become: namely, a sign, a foretaste, and an instrument of the kingdom of God? Too often we have focused our attention only within our walls.

Despite my own noble, long-preached ideals about pointing the church toward the world, I only learned this truth in full in 1983, when my wife was diagnosed with pancreatic cancer. Six doctors agreed she was terminally ill. No treatment anywhere seemed effective against this deadly form of cancer, so we explored any option, whether traditional or experimental.

When we visited the cancer clinic of Emory University Hospital in Atlanta, we discovered one doctor who specialized in radiation treatments. He combined radiation therapy with experimental deep heat therapy given by a physicist on the staff. My wife received the combination therapy for weeks. And, although she died shortly thereafter, I have always been deeply grateful to these two men who made every effort to save her.

Yet, imagine my initial astonishment when I realized the physicist performing the experimental dimension of this therapy had been a quiet worshiper in my congregation every Sunday! Not only that, he lived four houses up the street from us. What important work he was doing in cancer research, striving to develop a breakthrough on a deadly form of cancer! But until my wife's tragic experience, I confess I never knew what he was doing in the world.

While I hope my story is not typical, I fear it is for many ministers, particularly those in large churches. Would it not have been foolish for me to expect my physicist friend to expend most of his energy doing "church work"? Instead, *I should have spent more energy affirming him in his lifegiving work in the world as a servant of Christ.*

As leaders we must emphasize the crucial reality that Christians act as the *church gathered* and the *church dispersed*, a concept I first learned in 1961 from Reuel Howe. In the church *gathered*, we worship and are nurtured and equipped for our work in the world, the church *dispersed*. In other words, the church gathered acts as a service station, where our spiritual tanks are filled and our engines tuned to bring kingdom life to the world – where we spend most of our time.

As Christian leaders, we must keep addressing "the ministry of the laity" until, as a church, we get it right. Here are some guiding principles:

1. Ministry belongs to the whole people of God. "In a broken world," says *Baptism, Eucharist, and Ministry*, "God calls the whole of humanity to become God's people."[1]

2. All ministry in the church is a gift from Jesus Christ. Members, leaders, and ministers alike serve mutually under the mandate of Christ who is the chief minister of all. His ministry is the basis of all ministries; the standard for all of God's people is the pattern of the one who came "not to be served but to serve" (Matt. 20:28). The standard of *service* informs and undergirds the ministry that all of us do.[2]

3. Clergy and laity, ordained persons and unordained, share ministry. Each group has necessary and important tasks, differing only in function, not status.

4. "The Holy Spirit bestows on the community diverse and complementary gifts. These are for the common good of the whole

people and are manifested in acts of service within the community and to the world...All members are called to discover, with the help of the community, the gifts they have received and to use them for the building up of the Church and for the service of the world to which the Church is sent."[3] This notion of gifts bestowed by the Holy Spirit, though widely neglected, will become a building block for mission.

5. "God calls the Church in worship to join the mission of Jesus Christ in the world. As it participates in that mission the Church is called to worship God in Jesus Christ, who reigns over the world."[4] A profound rhythm exists between the church in its gathered life and the ministry of the church in its scattered life.

EQUIPPING THE CHURCH TO BE ALL IT CAN BE

The church partly equips members for their work in the world by meeting their basic needs. This requires leaders to be sensitive to the needs of people and open to the leadership of the Holy Spirit in discerning and meeting those needs. That means listening to people and listening to God – hearing the needs of others and prayerfully asking God to lend guidance as we make decisions.

Of course, these needs will be specific, particularized to each congregation and the persons who worship there. Yet, theologian Douglas John Hall identifies four overarching human quests: the quests for moral authenticity, meaningful community, transcendence and mystery, and meaning.[5] By briefly addressing each of these, we will point the way forward to the church's witness in the world.

1. The Quest for Moral Authenticity. When I first stepped into ministry, people in the United States were just beginning to slough off and discredit the "old morality," which was widely viewed as repressive, legalistic, dull, and negative. The Ten Commandments were considered hopelessly outdated, a relic, while the "new morality" was seen as open, loving, mutual, situational, realistic, and positive. With a battle cry to bring on the new morality, "all the people did what was right in their own eyes" (Judg. 17:6). And we plunged into a moral abyss.

While, granted, the old morality had its negative or incomplete dimensions, we now find ourselves in a moral lurch. Hence, the church must face the ethical dilemmas of our day, not retreat from them. We do that by examining our sacred biblical texts and traditions to discern how they represent and illumine our dilemmas today. What does the gospel say to marital partners torn between being faithful "as long as we both shall live" and "as long as we both shall love"? Or to an employee instructed to give kickbacks to potential customers because "everybody in the industry does it"? These dilemmas and others illustrate where many people "live and move and have their being."

So leaders and members, together, wrestle with these burning questions, seeking the mind of Christ. Such questions call us to our best critical thinking, our most fervent prayer, our most faithful communal support.

As leaders guiding people in ministry and mission, we must ask ourselves: Where is there space in our church life to deal with these problems? Do our sermons, Sunday school classes, youth groups, and Bible study classes help people in their difficulties? If not, the church can hardly be a sign to the world, a light to the nations.

The world does hunger and thirst for righteousness. But unless we satisfy our hunger and thirst in the gospel, we can hardly help the world in its longing. The quest for moral authenticity begins in the church itself.

2. The Quest for Meaningful Community. Many of us in today's church remain vaguely uncomprehending about the depth of community experienced in the early church – where members shared food and possessions and engaged in the strengthening graces of prayer and the Lord's Supper. So often today, struggling people come to our churches looking for deep community and the best we can do is put them on a committee.

God created human beings for community, and our rampant individualism, our go-it-alone strategy for living, only fails and frustrates. The world still longs for meaningful community. As church leaders, therefore, we must plan and work toward this atmosphere where "if one member suffers, all suffer together with it; if one member is honored, all rejoice together with it" (1 Cor. 12:26). This happens especially as we celebrate the sacraments, incorporating individuals into the family of God through baptism, and bringing people together around the table in the Eucharist.[6] When the sacraments are esteemed and practiced, God uses them in powerful, mysterious ways to unite us in Jesus Christ.

Church leaders also help form Christian community by providing for and encouraging small groups in the church where persons can study the Bible, pray, and find encouragement for ministry. When we as leaders experience the power of Christian community, we help shape this perspective in the church. As we lend enthusiasm to renewal services and faith discovery programs, we clear the path for ongoing renewal and community groups.

I witnessed the power of such groups firsthand some years ago, when a church I served conducted a five-week spiritual discovery program. For more than a month, small groups engaged in corporate and individual study of several disciplines of the faith, including prayer, Bible study, and fellowship. At the completion of the program, the congregation hosted a catacomb service to simulate the experience of Christians in ancient Rome. The sanctuary seemed strangely different in total darkness, resembling the catacombs in Rome where Christians worshiped in secret. The service alternated from sharing a scripture verse...to a prayer...to a song...to a brief witness. Toward the end of the service a man rose to his feet at the front of the sanctuary. I could hardly make out his frame in the darkness. But as soon as he spoke I recognized the voice of a man who had been in much difficulty. Quietly he said, "I had heard about love all my life but I never knew what it was until I saw it lived out among you people here." Then he sat down. About two weeks later he made a profession of faith, accepting Jesus Christ as Lord and Savior, and was baptized. In his life of turmoil he had longed for community but did not know what it was until the people in his group loved and accepted him as he was.

As Christian leaders we must make room in our congregations for these kinds of nurturing, faith-building, God-affirming groups.

3. The Quest for Transcendence and Mystery. At a conference in Pittsburgh, a Christian psychiatrist from Moscow – converted during the Communist regime in the former Soviet Union – gave testimony to his faith. Risking his state position (the atheistic government condemned all religious persons as psychotic), Sergei began quietly to explore an un-traceable "God nudge" in his spirit. A friend urged him to attend the Russian Orthodox Church and, finally, with the help of a priest, he claimed Jesus Christ as Lord and Savior – the fulfillment of his "God nudge."

God simply will not leave us alone! Even philosophers and scientists tease us with their speculations that the universe seems so incredibly purposive and intelligent that they ask: "How could such a creation exist without a God?"

Our technology has left us with marvelous gadgets and know-how but not the clue to our restless hearts. For all the incredible "answers" technology gives us, it offers no insight into transcendence and mystery – and the God question lurks beneath all our technological advances. We long for deeper communion with God and one another.

Church leaders must help members in this quest. We do this by asking, in dialogue with other leaders, how God has ended our own restlessness. Otherwise, how can the group meet this common need? We can provide space at each board or leadership meeting (or through retreats and other events) for leaders to be in touch with what is happening to them at the deepest levels of their being. *We must overcome the illusion that budgets, deadlines, buildings, and enrollment have more merit than cultivating a vital community which seeks and talks about God.* How tragic that the one organization founded exclusively upon the kingdom of God seldom makes space in its life for leaders to talk about their faith – or lack of it.

The quest for transcendence and mystery lingers in the minds of many people. Talk about it! Our faith in God, the Transcendent Mystery, anchors our witness of these things to the world.

4. The Quest for Meaning. In a Gallup poll on the spiritual needs of Americans, more than 70 percent of those polled identified the need for meaning and purpose as their number one concern.[7] Deep in our souls we hunger to know whether life makes sense; we daily confess with the Apostle Paul that "For now we see in a mirror, dimly" (1 Cor. 13:12).

We yearn for value and significance. Many persons seek to satisfy the quest for meaning by acquiring power or possessions, while others indulge in an endless pursuit of happiness by chasing one pleasure after another. And we are not satisfied!

Church leaders, who also quest for meaning, learn that we must not focus on what we *want* in life. Rather, we begin with God and concentrate on God's presence in the world, God's love for the world, and God's mission for our church. And we discover that when we do, God gives our lives meaning and purpose.[8]

We can learn from Kennon L. Callahan, who advises today's leaders as we seek to aid members in the search for value and significance. He points out that most of the understandings of the meaning of life that made sense in more agrarian and industrial civilizations have collapsed, at least at the local level. Into the vacuum left by the lack of clear consensus about goals and values has rushed a broad range of options, he says, but insisting on a singular view for everybody will not work in our current situation.

Nor will it help for church leaders to insist that everybody conform to our views as the "right answers." That will only bring more division.[9]

As a solution, we must help the local church to discover:

- its specific mission tasks in the world;
- its central convictions about everyday life in the light of the gospel; and
- who the church is now, on a mission field.[10]

Callahan advises us to discover our central convictions *after we explore our mission tasks* – realizing that, in opposition to our typical approach, our theology emerges as we wrestle with challenges right where our church is located.

Aware of our own wrestlings, we help church members become oriented to God – God's presence, love, and specific mission tasks for our church. We recognize that nothing less will end the quest for meaning and purpose.

Facing these four fundamental quests proves pivotal for all church leaders. These quests undergird our lives and the lives of those we serve, both in the church and the wider community. Addressing these quests is a large part of what it means to guide a church to be a sign, a foretaste, and an instrument of the kingdom of God.

QUESTIONS FOR FURTHER DISCUSSION

1. Do you think a hierarchy exists in the church, with clergy as first-class citizens, laity as second-class citizens? Support your answer.

2. As you listen to people talk in your church, what do you think they mean by doing "church work"? How much does your church leadership stress doing the work of the church in the world to actualize God's reign?

3. One church has imprinted on its bulletins: "Ministers: the Congregation." In what sense do you think this is true? Untrue?

4. How much emphasis should the church place on meeting the basic needs of people for moral authenticity, meaningful community, transcendence and mystery, and meaning? How does your church presently address those needs?

5. One contemporary church leader said that many Americans make their job their number one priority, their family second, their hobby third, and their church fourth. Do you agree? If so, what, if anything, can/should the church do about it?

CHAPTER 7

Finding and Using the Spiritual Gifts of Members

TED BABSON WAS
CHAIRING THE FALL
STEWARDSHIP DRIVE
AT FAITH CHURCH.
WHILE STUDYING THE
TIME AND TALENT
ASPECTS OF STEW-
ARDSHIP, HE BECAME
AWARE THAT HE KNEW
NOTHING ABOUT SPIRI-
TUAL GIFTS. "WHY
DON'T WE HAVE THE
CHURCH STUDY THE
BIBLICAL TEACHING
ABOUT SPIRITUAL
GIFTS?" TED ASKED
THE STEWARDSHIP
COMMITTEE. WHEN
THE COMMITTEE REC-
OMMENDED THE
STUDY TO THE BOARD,
IT PASSED AFTER A
SPIRITED DISCUSSION.
MOST BOARD MEM-
BERS ADMITTED THAT
THEY KNEW LITTLE
ABOUT SPIRITUAL
GIFTS.

As we seek to lead the church in becoming a sign, a foretaste, and an instrument of the kingdom of God, we must not only affirm the natural talents of members but also help them identify their spiritual gifts.

While both talents and gifts come from God, they vary in sometimes subtle ways. Talents may represent the means by which we express a gift of the Holy Spirit (1 Cor. 12:4-11, 27-31; Rom. 12:4-8; Eph. 4:11-16; 1 Pet. 4:7-12). The Holy Spirit bestows *gifts* upon all who have faith in Jesus Christ *for the building up of the body*, including, for example, teaching and exhortation. If God gives us the gift of teaching and we possess a talent, say, of relating and working with children, we may express the gift and the talent by teaching a third grade Sunday school class; if God gives us the gift of exhortation, of earnestly prodding the body to stronger faith, and also gives the talent of singing, we may express the gift through the talent by musically urging the community to hold firmly to faith.

Talents, however, are not designed exclusively for the building up of the body of Christ. We can sing in nightclubs as well as in sanctuaries, and we can work with children through community athletic teams as well as in Sunday school. And while we may build up the body in those non-congregational capacities, the gifts of the Holy Spirit are given specifically for building up the body of Christ.

It is the clear responsibility of church leaders to help members discover their gifts and to use them as God intended. What a difference it would make if the church devoted itself to this process, building ministry around the giftedness of members. We as leaders should focus on recognizing and developing the gifts of the Holy Spirit. We must be committed to this task, or there will be precious little discovery and development of gifts within the congregation.

SEEING OURSELVES AS THE BODY OF CHRIST

Let's examine Paul's rich material on spiritual gifts, drawing particularly from his invigorating analogy of the Body of Christ (1 Cor. 12:1-27) to consider the use and deployment of spiritual gifts. Explore this passage in-depth both individually and as a group to glean personal insights, tailored to a specific context. To launch such a discussion, consider the following insights.

1. The church, the Body of Christ, is corporate in nature. The church does not and should not represent a disconnected assortment of individuals who come together for occasional fellowship and worship without ties to one another or to Christ. It does not resemble a "beach bag" my family used to take on trips. In it I would throw a half dozen different items at the last minute…a can of tennis balls, an extra pair of shoes, a pair of sunglasses, a hat, a jar of roasted peanuts, a can of Gatorade. But those articles I tossed into the beach bag had no intimate connection with one another. I could take one out and throw it away, without losing anything of value to the other articles in the bag.

But it's not that way with the church of Jesus Christ. By baptism we were engrafted into Jesus Christ. And this means that when we were engrafted into Christ, we were incorporated into the church, his body. We cannot belong to one without belonging to the other. Therefore, those who say, "I have no need or use for the church" cannot be thinking in New Testament terms. We are members of one another, connected with each other for eternity and profoundly affected by each other.

2. Baptism makes one body out of the many members. "For in the one Spirit we were all baptized into one body – Jews or Greeks, slaves or free – and we were all made to drink of one Spirit" (1 Cor. 12:13). Imagine how striking Paul's words must have been to the Corinthians in the ancient world. Jews and Greeks were distant and historically despised one another; slaves were irrevocably set apart from free persons. Yet Paul says, "Jews or Greeks, slave or free" were baptized into one body and all were "made to drink of one Spirit." How shocking for the ancient world!

Yet when we are incorporated into Jesus Christ through baptism, we are also incorporated into his body, the church. And while, humanly speaking, we continually separate ourselves into various groups, building dividing walls of hostility, the Spirit forms all who come to Christ through baptism into one body. Paul's words remain astounding and promise-full to today's church.

3. All members of the body are valuable. The ear does not say, "Because I am not an eye, I do not belong to the body…" (1 Cor. 12:16). Every body part has a function, though not the same function. And every part has value, for it contributes to the function of the whole.

All members of the body should therefore appreciate the contribution every member makes and our own unique place in the body. Yet most of us struggle over our place. Many eyes – or should I say I's? – are not satisfied to be the eyes of the church body; they want to be the ears or the feet. They feel dissatisfied with the unique manner in which God has gifted them to participate in the very body of Christ. "God," Paul writes, "arranged the members in the body, *each one of them, as he chose*" (1 Cor. 12:18, italics mine). If God chose us to be eyes and not ears, then how can we refuse to be part of the body any longer? Instead we can say, "I am doing what God wants me to do, not what I have been asked to do." In other words, we more likely respond with enthusiasm and energy when the church benefits from our unique giftedness than when we grudgingly volunteer to fill some pre-established program need.

4. There are varieties of gifts, services, and activities within the body. "Now there are varieties of gifts, but the same Spirit; and there are varieties of services, but the same Lord; and there are varieties of activities, but it is the same God who activates all of them in everyone" (1 Cor. 12:4-6). To be complete, the church requires many different gifts, services, and activities, all set in motion by God's Holy Spirit.

From Paul's statement we learn at least two significant truths. First, God gives every church through its members whatever gifts God desires that church to have. And churches are gifted in quite different ways. No church can do everything. However, God has in mind for each church to do what its members are equipped to do…no more, no less. If a few members press the church to engage in a ministry for which no one has a gift, then the church's work will not go forward smoothly. Rather, it will spin its wheels and kick up mud as it travels contrary to God's intention.

Second, every member possesses a gift or gifts to be used in the body. All of us have gifts. By prayerfully examining the gifts identified in scripture, considering our personal strengths and joys, and soliciting the perspective of others in the body, we can determine the ways God has gifted and is gifting us.[1] The key for all of us remains to ask, "Am I using my gifts in the body of Christ?" How liberating to realize that God does not necessarily call us to contribute what someone else contributes. God only calls us to employ the gifts God has given us.

5. *"To each is given the manifestation of the Spirit for the common good"* (1 Cor. 12:7). Each gift we receive, each manifestation of the Spirit in our lives, is given to promote "the common good." Gifts do not promote our own glory; they do not let us lord over others; they are for the common good. The gifts promote love for God and neighbor, both in the church and in the world. The common good, then, involves building up the body, the church, and enabling members to minister to the world.

The appropriate use of our gifts to the church determines their value. For example, if my gift proves to be divisive, I must not be using it for the common good. If my prayer does not lead me to love God and neighbor more, something must be wrong with my prayer; and so with our gifts – we must exercise them for the common good.

After stressing spiritual gifts, Paul devotes great attention to showing us "a still more excellent way" (1 Cor. 12:31), the way of love. We may not be able to preach like Paul or serve like Mother Teresa, but we do have the capacity to love one another. And love always promotes the common good.

6. *The body is a caring body.* This passage reaches a climax when Paul says, "But God has so arranged the body, giving the greater honor to the inferior member, that there may be no dissension within the body, but the members may have the same care for one another. If one member suffers, all suffer together with it; if one member is honored, all rejoice together with it" (1 Cor. 12:24b-26).

In cyclical fashion, we see again the corporate nature of the church. Members of a body suffer with those who suffer, just as our bodies completely respond in sympathy when we have a toothache. We are not separated from the rest of the body but intimately connected with it. When someone in the body of Christ hurts, we hurt; when someone rejoices, we rejoice – for the church is a caring *body*.

A caring church does not stop loving at its own front door, of course. It moves into the community with the same caring spirit. We search for the hurts and needs of others whom Christ also loves. And then, through the giftedness of our own members, we reach out to heal those hurts in the name of Christ. The church remains, after all, the missionary body of Christ – and must be even more so in the years ahead.

Much of Paul's description flies in the face of contemporary, North American culture, which stresses individuality to the exclusion of the corporate – the significance of being "number one," the status of power, prestige, and possessions, and the desire for a flat, homogeneous church.

To meet the challenges of our changing world, however, we must draw from the biblical portrait, realizing that we are many, made one by the Spirit. The Spirit bestows gifts to all so we can work for the common good, manifesting a caring spirit for one another and the world. *So understanding our spiritual giftedness and our intimate connection with one another equips us for the challenges that lie ahead.*

THE HURTS AND HOPES
OF THE CHURCH COMMUNITY

We need another building block to flesh out this biblical approach to mission. As church leaders we must not only help members identify their spiritual gifts but also the specific hurts and hopes they long to address. Then we seek to intersect their gifts and longings with the hurts and hopes of the community. Kennon L. Callahan has popularized this approach.[2]

Callahan recommends that every church conduct a "mission analysis" of the community – *not* just a compilation of demographic data. By doing this, we seek to discover "(1) those major societal issues that are timely and pressing in the community; (2) those emerging groups likely to develop specific human hurts and hopes; and (3) the sense of the longings within given individuals and groups in the community at large to share concrete help."[3]

So the key to mission becomes *call*: discerning and matching gifts and desires with the hurts and hopes within the community. Callahan suggests that church members locate others who have similar longings and strengths with whom they can team in mission – addressing the community hurts and hopes identified in the above mission analysis.

As church leaders we must: prayerfully assist members to discern their gifts and callings; seek the hurts and hopes not being addressed in the community; seek to match persons with these hurts and hopes, helping them to find or form teams for mission; and help persons with other spiritual gifts to find a way to exercise their gifts for the common good. A person, for example, who discovers he has the gift of hospitality, might want to open his home to a visiting missionary couple. A woman who discovers she has leadership gifts might launch a small group for Bible study, prayer, and fellowship.

While such an approach recognizes that a congregation must limit its mission to the spiritual gifts of members, *the main goal for any church is to give itself away in line with the gifts God has given the church.*

As author Frederick Buechner suggests, we move toward finding the unique place and call of God for us as members and as a body *where our deep joy meets the world's deep need.*

QUESTIONS FOR FURTHER DISCUSSION

1. What difference do you think it would make in the mission of your church if you emphasized the spiritual gifts of members rather than recruiting members for specific jobs that have been predetermined?

2. What changes would your leadership have to make now and later to stress spiritual gifts?

3. How is your church similar to, and different from, the body image as Paul describes it?

4. As you think about your congregation, what examples can you find to demonstrate the corporate nature of the church?

5. Has your leadership ever determined specific hurts and hopes in the community? If you did, how would it change the way you do ministry?

Developing the Congregation's Mission

More than budgets and board meetings, the church needs spiritual mentoring and modeling from its leaders. We must take this challenge seriously as we seek to personally and corporately develop prayer, Bible study, ministry, and fellowship as foundations for our life together. Only by these methods and by the overarching guidance of the Holy Spirit can the church hope to become a sign, a foretaste, and an instrument of the kingdom of God.

Yet how do we "solidify" these things so they become concrete parts of church life? How can we use them to shape the congregation's mission? We must seek the Spirit's guidance in organization, leadership, and involvement of members. We begin by identifying spiritual gifts within the congregation. When members personally identify their gifts and we corporately affirm them, we begin to sense the "lay of the land" which God has mapped out for our unique congregation. In other words, gifts determine the type of ministry we can effectively fulfill. This proves vital as we try to discern God's call to us and to obey it.

To help determine what these gifts mean for our congregation, leaders should *involve members of the Body* in forming a mission statement. Ideally we solicit persons who have, for example, the gift of wisdom (1 Cor. 12:8), faith (1 Cor. 12:9), discernment (1 Cor. 12:10), ministry (Rom. 12:7), exhortation (Rom. 12:8), and/or leadership (Rom. 12:8) to help set in motion a formal statement expressing our understanding of God's call.

Next, we set down our understanding in writing so it remains before the congregation and before us as leaders as we make decisions. A board-appointed Mission Study Committee develops a "mission statement." Norman Shawchuck and Roger Heuser offer insights for developing a mission statement, suggesting that it contain:

- 125 words or less;
- A reflection of both vertical and horizontal relationships;
- Aspirations of the congregation while remaining realistic; and
- Meaningful, simple language without cliches.[1]

In addition, a mission statement should reflect an awareness of the gifts of members and the congregation's context for ministry. A sample mission statement from one local congregation appears below:

The Mission of Faith Church
Every member in prayer and ministry

God creates and calls us;
Jesus reconciles and redeems us;
The Spirit energizes and empowers us
for worship, love, and service!
In response to God's love and forgiveness, we pledge
to inspire each other to prayer, study, and stewardship;
to cultivate an open, caring church, where diverse gifts are
discovered, respected, and employed;
to minister faithfully to the poor, lonely, sick,
and those in need;
to reach out, sharing our faith, inviting and welcoming others
into our fellowship; and
to seek justice and healing in church, community, and world.

The above statement may appear deceptively simple. But every word, every phrase was studied, written, changed, and reflected upon in light of God's call of that church in its context, identity, programs, and processes.

Some persons may argue that the congregation wastes time in creating a purpose statement. They may object that each church's mission is clear: to preach, teach, heal, and serve...so why waste time developing new ways to say what the Bible has already told us so plainly? There are numerous reasons for engaging in the process and not merely adopting a pre-packaged mission statement.

1. Developing and refining a mission statement enables a church to pull together all of its understandings about the dynamics of its church life. It can then reaffirm the best of its past, discern God's call anew, consider changes, and move in new directions. Without concisely stating the church's mission, leaders tend to become discouraged and languish helplessly while repeating yesterday's programs.

2. A mission statement helps a church fully define its task. Otherwise culture (especially in these turbulent days) crowds the church so much that leaders lose sight of our reason for being. And we are likely to mount our proverbial horses and ride off in all directions! Without a defining mission statement, a church board may aimlessly nurse a church, not purposefully direct it to be an instrument of the kingdom of God. While serving several different congregations, I have found such a statement invaluable.

3. A mission statement helps a church to understand its own unique work by particularizing its mission. While every church is called to preach, teach, heal, and serve, no two churches will carry out that mission in exactly the same way. Each has a different identity and context, has different members who are equipped with different spiritual gifts, and belongs to a unique denominational heritage. Only by looking at all of these factors carefully can we discern what God wants our church to do at this particular time in our particular context.

4. A mission statement gives church leaders definite criteria by which to judge both short-term and long-term plans. When we as leaders establish goals for our work, we judge the validity of the goals by the mission statement. If a goal does not "fit," we should drop it – or we should revise the mission statement because of new insight.

But a word of caution is in order about mission statements. Once a church has drawn up an acceptable statement, its work has only begun! The mission statement offers a vision of what the church could be and do, but says nothing about how the church should get there. We take the next steps in light of the mission statement, knowing that goals and actions must follow.
To formulate goals and objectives, we must ask, "Given our calling, what can we do to fully express the life and ministry of the congregation?"[2] When church members voice conclusions and propose goals, we draw from our learnings any goals we wish to suggest.

In an effort to prioritize these goals we ask:

- What are the strengths of our church?
- What are some key issues we face, strategic decisions we must make?
- How can we help make a better world (nation, city/town, neighborhood)?

Our goals should express a quality of church life desired in the future. In writing goals, we do well to use verbs like *choose, decide, resolve, build, expand, serve, study, increase,* and *design.*[3]

Ideally, we devise goals which maintain a solid existing program; *strengthen* a weaker existing program; *add* vital new programs; and *remove* ineffective programs.[4] For example, if we were to discover a growing presence of senior citizens in the community, we might propose this goal: *To develop a comprehensive plan for enriching the lives of seniors in our neighborhood.* Next we reduce the goal into specific objectives to flesh out the intention. A sample objective for the goal about senior citizens: *By October 15, we will have in place a Meals on Wheels program to serve needy senior citizens in our community. By January 1, we will build a telephone network of callers to contact daily the elderly church members who do not live with extended families.*

Notice that the above objectives can be evaluated by the three-fold SAM test. Is it *specific?* Is it *attainable?* And is it *measurable?* If it fails in any of these areas, it should be sharpened until it meets all three criteria.

By claiming our unique call based on the spiritual giftedness of members, we recognize that we cannot meet all the goals and objectives we list – only those for which God has equipped the members of the body. Especially in a small church, goals should unify a church and focus it on a ministry that it can do well. In a large church, however, multiple goals provide a way for people from diverse backgrounds to participate in the church's mission.[5] When considering this planning model, small church leaders might be inclined to point out that the small church lives in a different world. They say, "When someone is hurting, we meet their need. When a job needs to be done in the community, somebody always steps forth. We don't need to set goals." Still, Carl Dudley has concluded that the goal setting process can be helpful in the small church "when 1) not everyone is expected to participate in the same way; 2) the identity from the past is unchallenged; 3) the present situation is seen as an opportunity, not a threat; 4) the decisions are not all made by vote; and 5) the responses are not all processed through organizational assignment."[6]

And yet, when we've identified the gifts of members, sought to discern the particular call of God for our congregation, considered the needs of the church and community, and developed goals and objectives, *we remain at the starting line.* Granted, we may have had a deep Christian experience and reached many interesting conclusions. Yet at this juncture, no ministry has taken place, no services have been conducted, and no programs have been initiated. We have performed vital, foundational groundwork, but we cannot quit here. By determining these things and implementing them, we lead the church in a new direction that will challenge and energize the congregation for years to come.

At this point we face two crucial tasks. First, we should appoint an ongoing mission committee to replace the Mission Study Committee. It discerns, filters, and assigns goals and objectives; monitors the progress of the work; and periodically reports to the leadership board. Second, we should determine whether to assign goals and objectives to new committees or to committees in existence.

First, an ongoing mission committee should contain several persons who have worked to determine the church's call and mission. *These persons should be freed from other board responsibilities, however, since this task is demanding.* What's more, every ongoing committee needs persons who participated in this study to provide continuity and background. It would be unwise to appoint an all-new, uninitiated committee.

Second, it may seem simpler and less threatening to assign responsibilities to existing committees. However, as church planners have pointed out, standing committees are notorious for routinely maintaining church as usual. They may even regard new proposals as a criticism of their previous work! Therefore, new goals and objectives may die a slow death, mostly through neglect.

On the other hand, most churches fail to have enough active members to start all new committees or task forces. If we find ourselves in this situation, we may want to combine the two approaches. At least the standing committees might be opened up to new members who want to work in particular areas. Where goals and objectives break new ground entirely, task forces can be appointed to handle the more detailed, comprehensive work.

A Supplemental Model

I am committed to the value of the mission statement approach in discerning God's will for a congregation. However, I am increasingly convinced that the entire process needs to be undertaken in an atmosphere of prayer for the guidance of the Holy Spirit. Early on we saw that the power of the Spirit gives collaboration a new dimension in the church. Surely this is also true for developing a mission statement. The Spirit enables the Mission Study Committee and the governing board to see what God wants each church to be and to do. Otherwise the process is likely to become mechanical, even dull.

Unfortunately, the church usually pays only lip service to the power of the Spirit as it is received in prayer. James C. Fenhagen relates a revealing encounter on a seminary campus.[7] A number of Christian denominations had gathered to participate in a continuing education event to deal with the church's response to the larger community. Given a controversial case study and asked to make a decision along denominational lines, each group met to decide how it would respond. One denominational group said that it would appoint a task force to work out a strategy to be voted on by the congregation. Another said it would present the controversy to its governing board and ask the board to decide. Still another announced that it would ask its bishop for a ruling on how to proceed. Fenhagen then reports, "Finally, after much discussion, a black Baptist pastor of a rapidly growing storefront congregation stood up to make his report. 'I don't understand where you all are coming from with all your talk about committees, strategies and task forces,' he said. 'In our church I would call all the deacons together and we would lock ourselves in a room and we would stay there praying until the answer came.'" Fenhagen reports there was nervous laughter in the room because other participants realized that the pastor had spoken a word they needed to hear.

"The storefront pastor," said Fenhagen, "had been talking about the gift of discernment and its place in the life of the church. It is a gift that the New Testament talks about frequently, but in our organization-minded church of today, discernment seems strangely out of place."

Is not discernment a gift of the Spirit that makes it possible for men and women to perceive God's will for them? Clergy and laity both have this gift. And, as Fenhagen further comments, "it is dependent on the collective wisdom of the whole church for its testing and verification. If we are to respond seriously to the unique gifts given to the church for its ministry, we are talking about discernment."

We note several important implications from the above insights. First, without earnest prayer for the Spirit to guide our planning processes, no discernment will occur. Second, discernment is dependent on the collective wisdom of the whole church for its testing and verification. Thus whatever proposals are made must be tested by the church for verification.

Now apply the gift of discernment in other ways. Individuals are given the gift of discernment, and remember that all spiritual gifts are given for the common good. Therefore when an individual perceives that God is calling him or her to initiate a certain ministry in the church, in the name of the church, that discernment must be placed before the corporate body for testing and verification. Suppose one member believes that God is calling her to initiate a ministry for the families of AIDS victims in the community. She then seeks out other persons in the church who feel a similar calling. Either the church as a whole, or its governing body, needs to verify the ministry as a valid gift of discernment if it is to become a ministry done in the name of the church.

Let's expand this thought. A growing number of persons expect that the church in the future will place greater emphasis on the ministry of small groups. Those groups will consist of persons who come together intentionally for nurture, worship, outreach, and mission. They will often discern God's will and will want to move out in ministry and mission to do God's will, supporting one another in their mutual ministries. Each time they propose a new ministry their discernment should be tested and verified by the congregation, either as a whole or through its governing body. The governing body, for example, might test the proposed ministry by the mission statement. The governing body can then say that the ministry fits well, or that it needs to be modified, or that the mission statement itself needs to be changed!

Thus, when developing a mission statement, the church can use management insights but should always seek the guidance of the Spirit. The Spirit will not only guide the process but will also grant the gift of discernment so that the church can perceive God's will.

A Summary of Leadership Responsibilities

Here is a brief description of the overall responsibilities we maintain as church leaders. By studying them we may acquire a proper perspective for developing a mission statement and setting goals and objectives.

1. Leaders commit themselves personally and the church corporately to prayer, Bible study, ministry, and fellowship.

2. Leaders help members identify the gifts God has given them for the upbuilding of the body.

3. Leaders draw on this giftedness in discovering God's unique call for this unique congregation – involving members in the process of forming a mission statement.

4. Leaders provide for and maintain a clear corporate vision for the congregation.

5. Leaders periodically ask themselves hard questions about the work. Among them: Are we as a board guiding this church to be a sign of the kingdom of God? Are we as a board modeling life in the kingdom, or merely reflecting the mores of society? Are we faithfully keeping the church leader pledge we have made? (See Appendix C.) Are we helping church members manage the messy situations in congregational life in light of the gospel story that gives us hope and meaning? While no leadership team can or should discuss all these questions at every meeting, these questions should appear from time to time on the board agenda.

6. Leaders supervise and evaluate the entire mission project as it develops. An ongoing committee more specifically oversees the project, but it needs to make periodic reports to the full board. When it does, the board needs to evaluate the quality of the work. Only then can we determine the appropriateness of the mission that has been approved.

QUESTIONS FOR FURTHER DISCUSSION

1. What is the unique call of your church? Has your leadership team discussed this or have you merely assumed it?

2. What would be the advantages of developing a mission statement for your congregation? What obstacles would you face?

3. Examine your church budget. What does it tell you about your real goals? How you spend your money?

4. Do you think the planning process contradicts the concept of building the church's mission around spiritual gifts and call? How are the two approaches compatible?

5. Do you have enough board members to allow some of them to be involved in a mission study committee?

Creating Changes

The Duke of Cambridge once said, "Any change, at any time, for any reason is to be deplored." And a church board member, who might well have agreed with the Duke, said, "Come weal or come woe, my vote is no!" Change is difficult for all of us. And, despite our best efforts as leaders, it also proves difficult for institutions, including the church. So the resistance to change should not surprise us.

The Mission Study Committee at any church needs to take note of this principle in planning to initiate change. No matter how good the change may seem to the committee, new proposals will elicit resistance.

Yet, resistance is not altogether bad. Indeed, church leaders traditionally function to put new proposals to the test and be convinced. We are called to prayerfully discern the need for any departures from the path.

On the other hand, as elders in my own Presbyterian tradition are charged in print, leaders must "lead the congregation continually to discover what God is doing in the world and to plan for change, renewal, and reformation under the Word of God."[1] So here we unveil the dilemma of being a church leader: on the one hand, we must guard the tradition, but on the other hand we must discover what God is doing in the world and plan for change, renewal, and reformation under the Word of God. This requires us to be innovative. As Shawchuck and Heuser put it, "Innovation is making change work for the good of the congregation, searching for change, and then exploiting it to fuel new ideas for new ministries."[2]

Testing new proposals in light of church tradition – where God has been active in the past – should then help leaders discern what God is doing in the world now. God, who through the Holy Spirit created the body of Christ, energizes and sustains the body. As Paul says, "There are varieties of activities, but it is the same God who *activates* all of them in everyone" (1 Cor.12:6, italics mine).

As we have seen, elders in the early church stood on a mission frontier, much as we do today. Daily they wrestled with broader issues than merely guarding the tradition against heresy and schism; they were also required to discern God's activity among them. While they did not form missionary societies as such, they certainly came to believe that the gospel existed for the whole world. For this reason, Paul and his friends fanned out across the Mediterranean basin. What's more, at the council meeting in Jerusalem, the apostles and elders decisively concluded that the gospel existed for all people. Gentiles were not required to live according to the law of Moses before being baptized and admitted to church membership. God was calling the church to do far more than conserve; God was calling the church to move into the future with an inclusive gospel for all humankind!

As we stand on a similar cultural precipice, we too must discern the call of God in our day and boldly move in new directions. The time has come for us as leaders to take more seriously our role "to discover what God is doing in the world, and to plan for change, renewal, and reformation under the Word of God." Today's missionary situation calls for renewal and change. How else can the church survive in an unchurched culture?

LEARNING FOR THE FUTURE

Chris Argyris and Donald Schön point out that organizations that respond best to changing societal conditions have three central governing variables.[3] They are strikingly similar to the principles of collaboration and supportive behavior we saw in Chapter 3. Effective organizations:

1. Generate valid and useful information. After any organization works to maximize valid information, it then presents this information to persons in a manner they can understand and use to make better decisions. Note the parallel to collaborative decision making in which all persons – not just a chosen few – are asked to contribute ideas and information to the decision-making process.

2. Provide for free and informed choice. All persons who will be affected by the decisions to be made are invited to participate in making the decision. They are given the gathered information regarding the pending issue to ensure that each person will make quality judgments. Note again the obvious parallel with collaborative decision making in which all persons participate in making decisions. Each church, of course, has to adapt this idea to its own type of governance.

3. Enlist internal commitment. The organization strives to enlist persons' commitment to the decisions. It also monitors what happens in order to provide information about the results of the organization's work. This principle once again demonstrates collaboration in action. When all persons contribute to the decisions affecting them, they will more likely commit themselves to the decisions made. Now, more than ever, it is crucial to involve church members in the planning process. After all, they are the heart and soul of the church and should participate at some level in the decisions that affect them. In no other way will they ever develop the internal commitment to live by and implement the decisions. Organizations that follow all three of the above principles show that they are learning organizations that can adapt to a changing world.

THE VARIABLES OF CHANGE

Every church board must wrestle with two change dynamics: internal changes, such as new members with creative ideas, and external changes, such as adapting the church's mission to its changing context. Facing external change proves more challenging for most congregations, yet addressing these changes will enable the church to remain vital and effective and to experience renewal *– because of the very changes that are taking place*. That cannot happen if we remain locked exclusively in a conserving mode. Every change proposed in a church can be assessed from within two dimensions: intensity and complexity. The following diagram from the Center for Parish Development depicts change according to increasing intensity and also the progressive difficulty church leaders may encounter.[4]

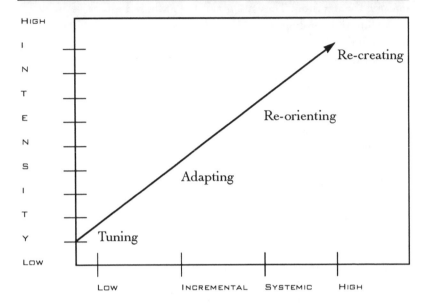

Let's examine these dimensions in detail.

Tuning changes are minor and incremental, made piecemeal in anticipation of future events. They are the least likely to produce trauma. Example: Having the church's furnace and air conditioner regularly serviced, not because there is a problem with either but to keep them running efficiently.

Adapting changes are also incremental but are made piecemeal in reaction to external events. To illustrate, the leaders did not anticipate the increasing number of senior citizens in the community. But now that the evidence proves overwhelming, the church adopts a "Meals on Wheels" program. Though this change fuels greater intensity than a tuning change, it is still not acute – it does not challenge or disrupt the harmony of the church.

Re-orienting changes move to a new level of intensity and complexity. Such changes are *systemic*, for, unlike incremental changes, they affect the organization as a whole. Not only are re-orienting changes systemic, but, like tuning changes, they also *anticipate* external events. Further, they impinge upon the church as a whole, asking people to make changes in 1) their perceptions; 2) their ways of thinking; and 3) their ways of behaving.

An example: A church committee prepares for the stewardship season by studying Douglas John Hall's book, *The Steward: A Biblical Symbol Come of Age.*[6] Committee members begin to see that stewardship is a revolutionary concept that touches the church at its very core if taken seriously. They want other members to see themselves as stewards (a synonym for "disciples"); they want persons to discover, as they have, that stewardship affects all of life. They conclude that stewardship is the mission of the church and not merely a means to mission. Over time they recognize this revolutionary concept as a re-orienting change, not merely a change touching one part of the church. This change in perception could spark enormous consequences in terms of how members think about themselves and act. Still, the committee neither intends nor foresees making any fundamental breaks with the church's core frame of reference. "The frame is bent but not broken," according to the theory.

Re-creating changes are also systemic, affecting the entire church. But they are reactive because the external events threatening the church were not anticipated. This requires radical breaks with the church's core frame of reference, including new leadership, values, strategy, power, influence, structures, and patterns of participation. In this case the church's frame of reference is "broken," not merely bent.

For example, a white middle class church suddenly finds itself located in a rapidly changing neighborhood. The church is totally unprepared for the change, does not want to see it, and suddenly faces a mass exodus of members fleeing to the suburbs. Attendance and the budget decline. The church can no longer maintain business as usual; radical changes are required in the church's mission and ministry. The immediate neighborhood becomes predominantly African-American within a few months. Desperate for help, the church appeals to the denomination, which urges the church to call an African-American pastor – especially since the white pastor has already moved on. The denomination also offers the services of its Urban Pastor to help the church identify the needs of the newly emerging community. Slowly the whole character of the church changes – its constituency, its style of worship, its outreach. It charts an entirely new direction.

Re-creating changes are the most difficult and complex to effect, requiring much outside help. I once pastored a church caught in similar circumstances to those I've just described. Not long after I became pastor, I discovered that the remaining members were aging and the least likely of all people to adapt to such swiftly changing conditions. As a result they yearned to "hold on" as long as they could until the church finally dwindled to a handful of people. In retrospect I can see that we reacted with *adapting, incremental* changes rather than the deeper surgery of re-creation that was needed. Incidentally, a few members have engaged in good ministry through the years – the church did welcome African-Americans who now number 20 percent of the membership – but frame breaking was required.

So church leaders, called to plan for change, renewal, and reformation, can learn from this chart. The more difficult the change, the more help we will need. Keep in mind that all systems resist change, even good changes. They want to stay the same! But in our changing world, when tremors of change ricochet in all directions, the church cannot simply dig in its heels. Today's situation offers unparalleled opportunities for learning and change – to be more fully a sign, foretaste, and instrument of the kingdom of God. To meet our future with confidence and grace, we must recognize the difficulty and complexity of change – underscoring our need to identify what is happening in our context.

While re-creating changes require outside expertise, here are some steps to guide us as we consider tuning, adapting, and re-orienting changes.

We must determine:

1. whether the change aligns with God's will as revealed in scripture. Is the proposed change in line with our mission statement? Will it help the church in a kingdom ministry?
2. the type of change, using the intensity-complexity diagram. Also, we must assess the difficulty of the proposed change.
3. who will be affected by it.
4. how to create structures that will involve the appropriate people.
5. possible resistances to the change and how we can deal with the resistances.
6. how to build a critical mass of key supporters for the change.
7. the best sequence for initiating the change process.[7]

THE POWER OF THE HOLY SPIRIT

Yet, as we have seen, the church is not just any organization but one *created* by the Holy Spirit, activated by the Holy Spirit, and *sustained* by the Holy Spirit. Not to seek the power of the Spirit in all situations is to separate the church from its source. Thus it is not enough for us to learn from secular theorists about the dynamics of change; rather, we must continue to rely on the church's ultimate source of power to discern God's will and to make God-ordained changes.

Whenever the church has successfully confronted internal and external changes, it has accessed the power of the Spirit. The oft-mentioned council meeting of the early church in Jerusalem (Acts 15:1-35) provides a stunning example of this point. At that crucial juncture, faith and culture stood at loggerheads as the council determined whether Gentile converts should be circumcised according to Mosaic law and whether Jewish and Gentile Christians, with vastly different dietary laws, should have table fellowship. (A *big deal* to the early church!) These issues brought Paul and Barnabas to Jerusalem to solicit the counsel of the apostles and elders and resolve the questions.[8]

The subject was undeniably controversial and guardians of "the way it's always been" would doubtlessly be inclined to squirm and fight to the death over these topics. But one thing prevented the collapse of the church at this fragile instant: *they sought the guidance of the Holy Spirit*. And what's more, they listened to it. "For it has seemed good to *the Holy Spirit* and to us to impose on you no further burden than these essentials..." (Acts 15:28, italics mine). They believed they were seeking the guidance of the Holy Spirit when they met, and they found it. Far from casually invoking the importance of divine guidance, the apostles and elders demonstrated this principle – willing to be pried from "the old ways" if God so led.

As proof of divine guidance, the assembly "*listened* to Barnabas and Paul as they told of all the signs and wonders that God had done through them among the Gentiles" (Acts 15:12, italics mine). Surely intent listening is a sign of the presence of the Spirit. And only by seeking the Spirit can we learn to listen intently and sincerely and show a willingness to be changed by what we hear.

Also, they "met together to consider this matter" (Acts 15:6). Apparently they invited open debate on the issues, looking for information and ideas from all, not just from early church giants like Peter, Paul, Barnabas, and James. And they arrived at a unanimous decision. "We have decided unanimously to choose representatives and send them to you..." (Acts 15:25). At least in some respects the council was acting collaboratively. The participants made decisions that were remarkable in their day.

What remains strikingly clear in Acts 15 is that the council made a momentous and harmonious decision that had far-reaching implications for the future of Christianity. In effect they decided that Christianity was for everyone, and that they weren't going to place the yoke of the law of Moses around anybody's neck. At the same time they encouraged the Gentiles to show respect for Jewish food laws, thereby making it easier for Gentiles and Jews to eat together. As Norman Shawchuck has said, "It was a dangerous moment in the life of the early church, but the people demonstrated that they could be in conflict without sin. And the Spirit of God never left them for a single moment."[9] *The meeting revealed that the Holy Spirit gave collaborative leadership a new power.*

QUESTIONS FOR FURTHER DISCUSSION

1. WHAT IS YOUR BOARD'S CONCEPTION OF ITS TASK — CONSERVING, OR WORKING TOWARD CHANGE, OR BOTH? EXPLAIN.

2. REVIEW THE CHANGES THAT HAVE OCCURRED IN YOUR CHURCH IN THE LAST FIVE YEARS. WHICH CHANGES WERE FORCED UPON THE CHURCH? WHICH ONES WERE PLANNED BY THE CHURCH?

3. OF THE VARIOUS KINDS OF CHANGE DESCRIBED IN THIS CHAPTER, WHAT KIND(S) DOES YOUR CHURCH NEED NOW?

4. HOW DOES YOUR BOARD TRY TO INCORPORATE CONTINUAL LEARNING IN ALL THAT IT DOES?

5. WHAT DID YOU LEARN FROM THE COUNCIL MEETING IN JERUSALEM THAT COULD INFORM THE LIFE OF YOUR BOARD?

Throughout these chapters I have painted in broad strokes how the church may prepare leaders for the future – and have suggested basic material to bring this to pass.

To summarize, we will focus on the unique call of God to the church. Then we will identify the spiritual gifts God has appointed within our congregation and respond to specific needs in the context in which God has placed us. Next we will attend to scripture and listen for God's direction – as well as listen to one another. In all these things we will strive to function as the body of Christ, becoming in every way participants in God's kingdom purposes.

Because of the longstanding marriage of our faith with North American culture, this approach seems dramatic. And indeed it is. Yet the old marriage of faith and culture is collapsing – if it has not in fact already collapsed – and we cannot continue business as usual. The contemporary context forces the Christian church on to a mission frontier.

Without question, this task requires careful attention. We must be bold and also humble; we must press forward and also pause to listen. Admittedly this proves difficult, for all of us are prisoners of the culture, trapped in its assumptions and misconceptions. And in many ways, even those of us who announce the coming of a new day may only dimly see how we should be the church in the new missionary situation.

Even so, we cannot continue leading the church as we have. The old ways simply aren't working anymore. New situations call for new thinking. Today's new thinking will return us to what historically has best informed the life of the church: a life grounded in Jesus Christ and a mission that calls the people of God to be kingdom people in faith and life.

With regard to the future, I am reasonably convinced of three things. First, the church will still require servant leaders who nurture their spirituality by opening themselves to the marvelous grace of God. If servanthood was the basis for everything Jesus did, surely it must be so for us.

Second, God will fashion us in new ways to reach out to all humankind to bring them to the unity and harmony God intends. Daily God works out the divine purpose, tearing down walls and building up people.

And third, *laity* will play an increasingly prominent role in the life of the church. They will do this by exercising their spiritual gifts to build up the church and extend Christ's loving mission to the world. They will emerge as the *primary players* in reaching out to humankind. As church leaders, we prepare laypersons to embody the kingdom of God in the world as we shift focus from the "church work" people do within the four walls of our congregation to the life-giving, life-sustaining work they do *in the world*.

I wish I could meet with your session, council, vestry, or diaconate. I would find it enriching to hear your dreams for the mission of your church, to see your members identify and employ their spiritual gifts, to watch you work together for the good of the whole church, to see you face conflicts creatively and hopefully, to join you as you pray fervently for God's presence in your lives and in the lives of your congregation. I believe daring congregations will provide exemplary models for the future mission of the church. Since I cannot meet with you, I can share these ideas with you, hoping you will study them, refine them, and revise them as you develop better ways of leading your church in ministry and mission. Above all, remember this: Old paradigms are breaking apart, new paradigms are being born. Yet God, our help in ages past and our hope for years to come, remains *with us* and always will be with us. In that promise lies our strength.

A RETREAT MODEL FOR SPIRITUALITY TRAINING

Friday Evening:

5:30-6:30 p.m.	Registration
6:30 p.m.	Dinner
7:30 p.m.	Opening Meeting
	Welcome *The Minister*
	Devotional *Church Leader*

Training Session I

I. The Nature of Christian Spirituality
 A. An Ecumenical Understanding
  1. The growth toward wholeness that God gives us in and through Jesus Christ and his kingdom and that manifests itself in loving care for God's creation.
  2. All spiritualities are true when they bring us – body, mind, and soul– into the presence of Christ, in the midst of a struggling and suffering world, and enable us to serve that world.
 B. Denominational Understandings
II. Sharing in Three's and Four's
 A. What or who was the source of your comfort and support as a child?
 B. When do you first remember thinking about God?
 C. Name a recent experience that has helped you grow in your relationship with God.
III. Types of Spirituality
 A. Evangelical Piety
 B. Charismatic Piety
 C. Sacramental Piety
 D. Activist Piety
 E. Academic Piety
 F. Ascetic Piety

G. Eastern Piety [1]
H. A Holistic Piety
   1. Balanced
      a. Fellowship
      b. Scripture
      c. Prayer
      d. Worship
      e. Service
      f. Witness
   2. Personal
   3. Corporate
IV. Closing Prayer

Fellowship Activities   9:00 p.m.

Saturday Morning

7:30 a.m.   Wake up
8:00 a.m.   Breakfast
8:45 a.m.   Opening devotional
9:00 a.m.   Training Session

Training Session II

V. Sources of Spiritual Growth
   A. Fellowship/koinonia/communion
   Have copies available of Acts 2:42-47. Write the following questions on the board for people to answer in groups of three or four.
     1. What was your first impression when you read this text?
     2. If you had been living in Jerusalem at the time, what would have impressed you most about this Christian community?
     3. To what do you attribute the difference between the Christian community today and the community described in this passage?
     4. What was the closest you have ever come to experiencing this kind of community?
     5. Where do you need the help and support of the Christian community now?
   Reconvene and share what you have discovered about Christian community.[2]

B. Scripture: Ways to Listen to God in Scripture
   1. Literal
   2. Allegorical
   3. Critical
   4. Contemplative
   Have Bibles available or copies of Mark 2:1-12. Guide the
   total group according to the following study plan:
      a. Read the text reflectively.
      b. Identify with a person or group.
      c. Imagine that you are present.
      d. Tell the story in your own words as though you
         were present.
      e. If you were present, what question would you ask
         Jesus?
      f. Write a dialogue with Christ.
      g. Write a short prayer.
C. Prayer
   1. Problems in prayer
   Make copies of the following statements, distribute them to
   the participants, and ask them to circle those that bother
   them most.

A PRAYER SURVEY

1. I wonder why I should pray when God already knows what I
   need before I ask.
2. I wonder whether my prayers actually influence God.
3. I wonder whether God really cares about the petty needs I have.
4. I wonder how God could possibly be concerned about all of our
   millions of prayers.
5. I wonder how I can discover God's will when I pray.
6. I wonder...

After participants have shared their answers in small groups, ask
them to return to the large group to share insights.

   2. A Model of Prayer (Put on an overhead projector and
   discuss each aspect.)

MEDITATE ON THE SCRIPTURES
After reading scripture, meditate on a key word or thought,
asking God to speak to you.

PRAISE GOD
Praising God for who God is prepares the way for every aspect of prayer that follows.

MAKE CONFESSION
The moment we come into God's presence we realize that we fall short. Yet we can confess our sin, knowing that God forgives us.

GIVE THANKS
Thanking God for our blessings each day enables us to approach life with the right perspective.

PRAY FOR OTHERS
Though we do not understand how intercessory prayer works, we pray because Jesus taught us so to pray and also because we believe that our loving God cares about us.

OFFER PETITIONS
We are dependent upon God as the source of our life. How natural then it is for us to ask God for what we need!

TRUST GOD
The God who created the universe, the God of our Lord Jesus Christ is one who can be trusted to hear our prayer and answer it according to the divine will.

PRAY "OUR FATHER..."
Jesus taught his disciples to pray the Lord's Prayer. What a fitting way for us to conclude our prayer time.[3]

10:30 a.m.   Mid-morning break

Training Session III
D. Worship (The questions that follow are for private and small group reflection.)
   1. Praising and loving God
       a. Upon what do I focus the hottest intensity of my mind?
       b. When did God become more than a word to me?
       c. What keeps me from loving God with all my heart,

soul, mind, and strength?

    d. What do I most need help with in my relationship with God?

2. Enhancing personal worship

    a. What practice or discipline would most enhance my personal worship?

    b. What practice or discipline do I need help with right now?

    c. How can I become more accountable for my personal worship?

3. Enhancing household worship

    a. Do I worship with my family? If so, how?

    b. Do I ever talk about matters of faith with my family?

    c. How can we as a family begin to worship together?

    d. What is the connection between family relationships and personal faith?

4. Enhancing public worship

    a. What is my earliest memory of public worship?

    b. How often and under what circumstances do I engage in public worship?

    c. What part do the Sacraments play in my understanding and appreciation of worship?

    d. What is the connection between my worship on Sunday and my work on Monday?

12:30 p.m.   Lunch

1:30 p.m.   Reconvene

Training Session IV

E. Service: The Result of Loving God

Ask people to share first in triads, then the larger group.

1. Whom do you have difficulty loving?

2. Who needs your love now?

3. What prevents you from loving others as Christ has loved you?

4. Who needs our church's love in this community?

5. What prevents us from loving them as Christ has loved us?

F. Witness: The Love of Christ Controls Us

Share first in triads, then in the larger group.

1. Who most influenced you to follow Christ? Describe that person.
2. Whom do you know who needs the gospel right now?
3. What, if anything, is preventing you from witnessing to that person in word and/or deed?
4. What support do you need from others to grow in your ability to witness?

3:30 p.m.   Closing Worship

Suggestions for Developing Collaborative Skills

1.Supportiveness

Divide participants into triads, one to role play as the Church School Superintendent, one as a sixth grade teacher, and one to be an observer. The roles are as follows:

Teacher: You teach a sixth grade class of boys and girls. Three boys, two of whom are sons of influential leaders in the church, sit together, do not pay attention, and disrupt the rest of the class. You are exasperated to the point of quitting. As a last resort, you schedule a conference with the superintendent who recruited you for the job.

Superintendent: Your role is to listen, communicate acceptance, and be as supportive as possible.

Observer: You are to note what goes on in the interaction. Is the superintendent acting supportively? listening carefully? communicating acceptance?

After a few minutes participants should end the role play and debrief. The teacher and superintendent should first share how they felt during and after their talk. Then the observer should share his or her notes. What lessons did you learn about practicing supportive behavior?

If time permits, switch roles and repeat. For the sake of variety you may want to make the teacher's role one of leading an adult class that desires only straight lecture.

2. Openness and Receptivity

Divide participants into triads for a role play, one to be the pastor, one a church member, and one an observer. The roles are as follows:

Member: You have searched to select an appropriate memorial gift for your father who died a year ago. You remember how fond he was of the King James Version of the Bible. You eagerly approach your pastor in the hallway one day, saying you want to buy a King James Version of the Bible for the pulpit in memory of your father.

Pastor: You remember that the pulpit Bible, a New Revised Standard Version, was recently purchased. You strongly believe that the NRSV is not only more accurate than the KJV but much more understandable. Your role in the conversation is to affirm the person, look for any merit in his or her idea, and at the same time be yourself.

Observer: You are to see how open and receptive the pastor is to the member's new idea. What feelings does he or she communicate to the member? Is the pastor able to affirm the person and yet retain his or her own integrity? Does he or she relate so as to maintain the relationship with the member?

After five minutes or so, participants should debrief the exercise. The pastor and member should first share their impressions of the conversation, followed by the observer. What did you learn about being open and receptive to others? You may want to switch roles and repeat the activity.

3. Team Development

Purpose: to build ourselves as a team through a process of looking at the way we would hope to work together.

Setting: assemble committee chairpersons and committee members in a large room. Then instruct persons to meet with their committees.

Step I: Each chairperson will take a piece of newsprint and list how he or she would hope to work with committee members using these categories:

| *Things I would hope to do* | *Things I would hope the committee members would do* |

Step II: (At the same time) The committee members will meet together and list on newsprint how they would hope to work with the chairperson using these categories:

| *Things we would hope the chairperson would do* | *Things we would hope we (as committee members) would do* |

Step III: Chairpersons and committee members together compare the lists. Ask:

1. What are the specific points of similarity?
2. What are the specific points of difference?

3. What are the assumptions behind these two lists?

4. What do we need to do to work together more effectively back home in light of our expectations?

Note: I adapted this exercise from one used in a workshop with Robert Worley of McCormick Theological Seminary.

4. Helping Members with Their Work

Divide participants into triads, one to be the pastor, one the Chairperson of the Worship Committee, and one to be an observer. The roles are as follows:

Chairperson: You will conduct your first committee meeting in a few days. You have never chaired a meeting of this type before, yet you have admired the way your pastor has presided over meetings of your governing board. The pastor seems to know how to run a meeting. You make an appointment, go to the pastor's study, and seek to learn some of the same skills the pastor has.

Pastor: Your role is to show the chairperson that you are available and want to help.

Observer: Your role is to note whether the pastor is helping the chairperson. Is the pastor willing to help, to share useful information, to identify resources? Would the chairperson likely call upon the pastor for help in the future?

After five minutes or more, debrief. First, let the pastor and chairperson share how they felt, followed by the observer. What did you learn about helping members with their work? Reverse roles and repeat.

5. Expecting Excellence from Members

Divide participants into triads, one to role play the Chairperson of the Nominating Committee, one a person who the chairperson will approach to coordinate all volunteer services in the church, and one to serve as an observer. The roles are as follows:

Chairperson: You want to stress the importance of the job you are asking the person to take.

Member: You are simply to be yourself, responding as you think you truly would to the chairperson's presentation.

Observer: You are to make notes on the conversation. Did the chairperson reduce the importance of the job in order to receive an affirmative answer? Did he or she talk about the job in such a way that the member would desire to do it well? Did the chairperson also communicate an understanding of the member's situation, including feelings involved?

After five minutes, debrief, allowing the chairperson and member to speak first. Then the observer will share impressions of whether the chairperson expected excellence in the member's work. What, if anything did you learn about the importance of expecting excellence?

6. Group Methods of Decision Making

Place an ordinary brick (preferably one with holes in it) in front of the entire group. Give participants two minutes to think of all the possible uses they can determine for the brick.

Next, divide the participants into groups of four. Ask them to pool their knowledge about the possible uses for the brick.

Finally, reassemble the entire group. Ask how many uses persons arrived at individually. Next, ask each group to share their total number of uses. Lastly, discuss the number of uses the whole group developed, comparing the number to the group and individual totals. Stress how groups, using their individual and corporate resources, can come up with more input and better decisions than an individual working alone. *"No one of us is as smart as all of us."*

A CHRISTIAN LEADER'S PLEDGE

A Christian Leader's Pledge

Recognizing that God has called me by providence to serve as a leader in the Church, Christ's body, and that the Holy Spirit empowers me to live a life of witness and service among God's people and in the world, I pledge to govern my life by observing certain practices I have chosen.

Knowing the Gospel:

1. Daily I will study the Scriptures, our authority for faith and life, to help me love, know, understand, and obey God.
2. Daily I will study both my tradition and the Christian tradition to discern God's movement in history.
3. Daily I will think about the needs of the world, especially the needs of the poor and oppressed, in light of the gospel of Jesus Christ and will reflect on what the church and I can do to meet those needs.
4. Whenever church meetings require my leadership, I will seek to be present and prepared. I will work with my colleagues with love, respect, and support.

Being the Gospel:

5. Each day I will engage in prayer to almighty God, offering myself to God as a servant.
6. At least weekly I will worship with God's people, taking particular advantage of opportunities to commune with Jesus Christ in the Lord's Supper.
7. I will seek out persons or a person with whom I can share my life and receive their wisdom about the movement of God's Spirit in my life.
8. Periodically I will make a personal spiritual inventory that covers these points:

a. What kind of person does God want me to be?

b. What gifts has God given me that I may use in the service of God's kingdom?

c. In what ways does God want me to use my life?

d. What stands between me and the will of God?

Doing the Gospel:

9. I will remember that I am a servant of Jesus Christ, chosen to witness and bear fruit in my home life, workplace, and community activities.

10. I will be accountable to my colleagues in leadership positions for the faithful performance of my duties and for the practice of these disciplines.

11. Daily I will think about and pray for the people of the church I am leading, and seek to work among them with energy, imagination, and love.

12. I will strive to be aware of, and seek to influence, systems and structures in society that oppress people and deny them the opportunities of life that I enjoy.

AN AGENDA FOR SPECIAL QUARTERLY MEETINGS

Note: Most boards do not have enough or provide enough time to deal with the following material at regular monthly meetings. Therefore, some boards have adopted special quarterly meetings to deal with substantive matters in a less pressing atmosphere. The following suggestions are drawn from the quarterly meetings of the Faith Church board and should serve to prime the pump for your quarterly meetings. These meetings are yet another way to appropriate any insights you have gained.

SUGGESTIONS FOR USING APPENDIX D

1. Let the way the quarterly meetings flow at Faith Church in the following scenarios stimulate your imagination about conducting a similar meeting with your own board.
2. You may use the discussion of the meetings more or less as case studies and invite the board members to respond to them. Here are relevant questions to ask about each:
   a. What did Faith Church do that makes me uncomfortable and resistant? Why?
   b. How did the agenda for the Faith Church quarterly meetings differ from our board meetings?
   c. What did Faith Church do that I would like to see us try in our church?
   d. What do we need to do to get started?

First Meeting: The first special quarterly meeting to revitalize the board's working relationships deals with becoming accountable to one another. Appendix C contains "A Christian Leader's Pledge" to which each leader is invited to respond. But each leader will then need to be accountable for the aspects of the pledge to which he/she has committed himself or herself. The first meeting addresses this need in terms of prayer, which is likely to be a discipline most leaders will choose. See further the content on prayer in Chapter 2. Here is a possible way to structure the meeting.

Introduction: The one presiding may offer an honest, personal statement such as: "I still struggle with the amount of time I devote to my personal disciplines. When I get busy, I think I don't have time to pray. How is it with you?"

Sharing: Ask for the board's responses as a total body (if the board is small) or in two's or three's if the board is large.

Possible Responses

Response #1: "I find that it's easier for me to read books on prayer and to talk about it than it is to pray! When I realized what was happening to me, I simply started praying more without beating myself to death with guilt."

Response #2: "I've found it helpful to expand my understanding of prayer. Roberta Bondi says that when we practice loving ways of being, we are praying.[1] Now that was a new slant on prayer for me. The other day I realized that I had been very irritable over the weekend with my wife, and that she had done nothing at all. It was a matter of my own inner stress and unhappiness. So I apologized to her. It was amazing how much better she and I both felt after that. As Bondi says, doing that which moves us toward love for another person is a necessary part of prayer.[2]

Response #3: "I've discovered that following set times of prayer is difficult for me. I know I need to explore how to do that in more depth. But in the meantime I've been praying more spontaneously during the day. I often get caught in traffic jams coming to work. I have been turning off my radio. Instead of fuming at other drivers the way I used to do, I've been rhythmically praying a verse from a psalm. "Be still and know that I am God" is my favorite. It keeps me focused on what I'm about as a Christian and also makes me a lot more patient with irritating drivers!"

Response #4: "Roberta Bondi also says that the goal of the Christian life is love of God and neighbor and that prayer plays an important part in learning to love.[3] It seems to me that your meditation in traffic is helping you to do just that. Perhaps we ought to measure all of our prayer methods by this test: Are they increasing our love for God and neighbor?"

Becoming More Accountable: The one presiding next invites the board members to become more accountable for their prayer life. He or she suggests that each leader draw a name from a pile of names of other board members. The leader then prays for that person until the next meeting when the process is repeated. The person is encouraged to call the person for whom he or she is praying to determine prayer needs.

Second Meeting: The purpose of the second quarterly meeting is to encourage leaders to address evangelism. The meeting revolves around three questions that open up the subject for the leaders. The one presiding asks the following three questions:[4]

Question A:

"What do you see or hear in the lives of people with whom you live and work that reveals a hurt or longing for which the gospel might be intended?"

Possible Responses

Response #1: "There's a woman who works in my department at our electronics plant. She's so quiet you hardly know she's there. Most of my co-workers simply avoid her. They say she's hard to get to know. But I know she's lonely. I can see it in her eyes. Guess I haven't done anything about it, though."

Response #2: "I've got the opposite situation. In my unit there's a man who never stops talking. Behind his back we call him 'Motor Mouth.' Nobody can stand to be around him, so we avoid him like the plague. But I know he's reaching out for help and doesn't know how to find it."

Response #3: "My son plays Little League baseball, and I attend all his games. There's another woman at the games who is really obnoxious. She yells at the umpires constantly, groans when her son is not in the game, and turns everybody off. I don't know whether the players hear her or not, but believe me, we sure do. And it drives me crazy."

Response #4: "We've got a manager in our company who thinks of nothing but the bottom line. I mean nothing. If I increase my sales 25 percent over the previous year, he tells me that I must go out and do it again. Of course, it's impossible to do that every year. At our last sales meeting, one of our reps told him that every salesperson in the room was working to the max and for him to quit putting so much pressure on us. But I don't think it has done a bit of good. He is definitely expressing a hurt or need for which the gospel is the answer."

Question B:

"What was the human cry in you that responded to the gospel?"

Possible Responses

Response #1: "This is painful for me to admit, but I've always been big on control. I've wanted to control everybody in my family and on the job, too. And if anything went wrong, I usually knew someone who could fix it...I had many connections. But when Jane, our daughter, was hit by a car five years ago, all of my control mechanisms went out the window. For days my wife and I didn't know whether she would live or die. For the first time in my life I was up against something I couldn't fix. I felt helpless, almost broken. I had to depend on God and my friends in a new way, as a needy, helpless human being. When Jane did pull through, I was a different person. Not only did she recover, but I think I began to recover also – recover from the 'I'm in control of everything' syndrome."

Response #2: "I retired two years ago after working at GM for thirty-five years. They gave me a nice party and the traditional fancy watch. But for the first six months of my retirement, I almost went crazy. I played golf every other day and watched television at night. Even took a nice trip or two. But I was miserable. I wasn't producing anything anymore! Besides, as much as I had complained about it at the time, I missed the gang at work. I faced a real crisis about what I was going to do with my life. It was then that I signed up for our tutoring program at the prison. I'll have to admit that, for awhile, I was more worried about myself when I retired that I ever was while I was working. I began to hear the gospel in a new way."

Response #3: "For a long time after Frank and I married, everything came up roses. Here I am, eight years and two children later, and my perspective has changed drastically. I've always been a perfectionist. The kitchen and the house must be spotless. Children always have to say please and thank you. Mom has been sick off and on for three years. Life has simply destroyed my ability to do everything right. The house is sometimes a wreck, my children aren't perfect little angels, and I'm not pleasant to live with. So I've had to admit my need for help, both to God, to Frank, and to others."

Response #4: "When Phil and I had been married ten years, I received a dreadful phone call one night. I was informed that Phil had been in a wreck, was rushed to a hospital in Charlotte, but was dead on arrival. I remember asking out loud, 'What will I ever do without Phil? How can I make it with these two small children?' I cried out for help any way I could find it. I had to go back to work to make ends meet and get day care for the children. What a struggle it was! Some days I just asked God for the strength to get me through that one day. And God did. The days have stretched into the years now, and by God's grace I have made it."

Question C:
"Realizing what a treasure we have in our minds and hearts, what keeps us from sharing it with those around us?"

Possible Responses

Response #1: "I think most of us believe a person's religion is a private affair and that we shouldn't intrude with our faith. I know that's wrong, but I'm sure it blocks me sometimes."

Response #2: "I'll have to admit that I have simply been very uncomfortable talking to anyone about my faith. And it's so strange, because I know that my faith in Christ is the only thing that has seen me through the last few years."

Response #3: "I also have some of your reluctance to share the gospel, but I decided to begin where I could. I asked God for strength to move from there. I started by trying to get to know the man I called 'Motor Mouth.' I'll have to admit that I didn't want to do it. But the more I came to know his story, the more I understand why he tried to keep everyone at arm's length. Gradually I became comfortable enough to invite him to our church one Sunday. He wouldn't come, though. Said it was too far away for his children. Yet he did become active in a church nearer his home. I can now see a slow change taking place in him."

Response #4: "I used to be in a Bible study group about three years ago. As we shared our stories around a Bible passage week by week, I found that it was much easier to talk to people outside the church. I knew that every person in that group had a deep need, and that everyone else did too. So I no longer hesitate to pick up on the feelings of others and try to relate the gospel to their needs. And every time I do it, I become a little more comfortable."

Conclusion

After the group has shared thoroughly (but with no pressure placed on anyone to share), the one presiding should summarize the group's input on evangelism. Then the board can brainstorm ways to hold one another accountable for witnessing to the gospel, summed up in the pledge as follows: "I will remember that I am a servant of Jesus Christ, chosen to witness and bear fruit in my home life, workplace, and community activities."

Third meeting: The purpose of this meeting is to explore the board's work in light of the church's need to be a sign, foretaste, and instrument of the kingdom of God. The immediate problem facing the board: How to respond to the request of the senior high youth group to add a small room to the Mexican church at Merida.

How the Board Responded

Problem #1: The discussion first revolved around whether or not the trip was in line with the church's mission statement. When they looked at their statement they concluded that the trip was certainly in line with their mission as they understood it. It plainly stated: "The Spirit energizes and empowers us for worship, love, and service."

Problem #2: How would the church finance the trip? The first proposed solution was to have Saturday car washes. However, this time they approached the problem differently. Someone asked, "Does the fact that we are a sign, foretaste, and instrument of the kingdom of God affect our decision?" They decided for a number of reasons not to lean on the community to support their effort. They reasoned that it was the wrong message to send to the community, especially since they would have been competing with a commercial car wash in the next block that had to pay taxes. An altogether new solution emerged. They developed a plan to enlist sponsors within the church for the trip, to whom the youth would write during their trip and for whom they would cook a pancake breakfast upon their return.

Problem #3: How could the board demonstrate collaborative planning instead of doing all the planning for the youth? They decided that they would ask two board members to meet with the youth to get their feedback on the plans and to report at the next regular meeting.

Fourth Meeting: The purpose of this meeting is to improve board functioning. The board had discovered that they were not really collaborating around specific missional issues. Rather, the Christian Education Committee met to further its work and to protect its own turf. The Worship Committee did the same for its work. They had no sense of working together to contribute to the whole; they had been leaders of specific areas, not servants of the total mission.

Possible Responses

Response #1: "I think we ought to let our mission determine the actual work our committees do. For example, our new mission statement says that 'we pledge to cultivate an open, caring, and inclusive church family where we discover, respect, and employ our diverse gifts.' We spelled that out a little more by saying we could target our worship, programs, and outreach to groups of people who work or live in our community and who can be touched by persons in our church as they employ their particular gifts. What would happen if we let each one of our committees work on how it could contribute to that goal?"

Response #2: "We have targeted three groups of people, first, visitors, parents with babies, parents with older children, and retirees. Second, the international community, those working in the area who drive by our church, and new people working in the community. And third, singles. Each committee could work on what it could do to reach each one of those particular groups."

Response #3: "Since I chair the Spiritual Gifts Committee, we would first need to help our members identify their gifts and concerns. We would next identify the hurts and concerns of the target populations we have specified in our community. Then we would try to match gifts with needs."

Response #3: "Our Spiritual Life Committee could work on how we can best meet the needs of our targeted groups for prayer, Bible study, and small groups. What are their needs for community and meaning?"

Response #4: "Our Christian Ed Committee might attempt to work out a ministry based on the parenting needs of the targeted group. Or the needs of the singles."

Response #5: "Our Worship Committee can begin to look at our services from the perspective of those people we have targeted as a result of our mission statement. For example, how would a typical single in our community view our worship?"

Response #6: "It looks as if we have agreed to focus our committee work on how we can best contribute to the mission goals we have adopted. What we have talked about is a re-orienting change. It will involve changing our patterns of thinking, feeling, and doing. So we need to do some additional work on how we will enable our committees to see the vision we are now seeing."

Chapter 1: Serving to Lead

1. Thomas C. Campbell and Gary B. Reierson, *The Gift of Administration: Theological Bases for Ministry* (Philadelphia: The Westminster Press, 1981), p. 71.

Chapter 2: Becoming a Community of Leaders

1. Norman Shawchuck and Roger Heuser, *Leading the Congregation: Caring for Yourself While Serving the People* (Nashville: Abingdon Press, 1993), p. 47.
2. Ibid., p. 47.
3. "Here, O Our Lord, We See You Face to Face," *The Presbyterian Hymnal* (Louisville, KY: Westminster/John Knox Press, 1990), no. 520.

Chapter 3: Learning to Work Together

1. Charles H. Ellzey and Paul M. Dietterich, eds., co-written with Norman D. Self, "Leadership Styles for Productivity and Member Satisfaction," *The Center Letter*, 6 (April 1976).
2. Based on the work of the Center for Parish Development in Chicago, IL.
3. The Center for Parish Development, *Leadership Skills for Effective Ministry*, (Naperville, IL: The Center for Parish Development, 1979), Module 3, Topic 4, p. 2.
4. See Lawrence O. Richards and Clyde Hoeldtke, *A Theology of Church Leadership* (Grand Rapids, MI: Zondervan Publishing House, 1981), pp. 106-109.
5. Alvin J. Lindgren and Norman Shawchuck, *Let My People Go: Empowering Laity for Ministry* (Nashville: Abingdon Press, 1980), p. 47.

6. Charles H. Ellzey and Paul M. Dietterich, "Leadership Styles for Productivity and Member Satisfaction: No. 3 The Leader Who Emphasizes High Quality in Performance," *The Center Letter 6* (July 1976).
7. Rensis Likert, *New Patterns of Management*, (New York: McGraw-Hill Book Company, 1961); also by Likert, *The Human Organization*, (New York: McGraw-Hill Book Company, 1967).

CHAPTER 4: FACING THE CRISIS BEFORE THE CHURCH TODAY

1. Edward A. White, "Pastoral Transitions for Learning and Growth," *Inside Information X* (Summer 1992): 4. He credits Joel Barker's video, The Business of Paradigms: Discovering the Future (Burnsville, MN: Charthouse Learning Corporation, 1990), for this example.
2. Loren B. Mead, *The Once and Future Church*, (Washington, D.C.: The Alban Institute, 1991), p. 12.
3. Ernest Trice Thompson, *Through the Ages: A History of the Christian Church* (Richmond: The CLC Press, 1965), p. 28.
4. Stanley Hauerwas and William H. Willimon, *Resident Aliens* (Nashville: Abingdon Press, 1989), p. 18.
5. William Butler Yeats, "The Second Coming," *The New Oxford Book of English Verse* (Oxford: Oxford University Press, 1989).

CHAPTER 5: DEFINING THE BASIC LEADERSHIP TASK

1. I am particularly indebted to the Center for Parish Development for this guideline. See *A Systems Model of the Church in Ministry and Mission*, (Chicago: The Center for Parish Development, n.d.).
2. John B. Cobb, Jr., "The Holy Spirit and Leadership by Proposal," unpublished paper, pp. 3-4.
3. Ibid.
4. See Paul S. Minear, *Images of the Church in the New Testament* (Philadelphia: The Westminster Press, 1960).
5. Paul D. Hanson, *The People Called: The Growth of Community in the Bible* (San Francisco: Harper & Row, 1986), p. 467.
6. Minear, *Images of the Church in the New Testament*, p. 68.
7. Ibid., p. 69.

8. Walter Brueggemann, *Genesis* (Atlanta: John Knox Press, 1987), p. 1.

9. Robert H. Ramey, Jr., *The Minister's Role in Evangelism* (Decatur, Ga: CTS Press, 1985) p. ll.

10. The Center for Parish Development, *A Systems Model of the Church in Ministry and Mission*, (Chicago: The Center for Parish Development, n.d.), p. 30.

CHAPTER 6: SHARING THE VISION WITH CHURCH MEMBERS

1. *Baptism, Eucharist, and Ministry* (Geneva, Switzerland: World Council of Churches, 1982), p. 20.

2. Presbyterian Church (U.S.A.), *Form of Government, Book of Order*, G-6.0101. (Cited hereafter as *Book of Order*.)

3. *Baptism, Eucharist, and Ministry*, p. 20.

4. Directory for Worship, *Book of Order*, W-7.1002.

5. Douglas John Hall, *An Awkward Church*, (Louisville, KY: Presbyterian Church (U.S.A.), 1993), p. 22.

6. Jackson W. Carroll, *As One With Authority: Reflective Leadership in Ministry* (Louisville, KY: Westminster/John Knox Press, 1991), p. 106.

7. Marjory Zoet Bankson, "Not Home Alone," *Faith at Work 106* (Jan/Feb 1993), p. 2.

8. See *Theology and Worship Ministry Unit*, Presbyterian Church (U.S.A.), Growing in the Life of Christian Faith, *Report to the 201st General Assembly* (1989), (Louisville, KY: 1989), p. 3.

9. Kennon L. Callahan, *Effective Church Leadership: Building on the Twelve Keys* (San Francisco: Harper & Row, 1990), pp. 117-123.

10. Adapted from Callahan, *Effective Church Leadership*, p. 122.

CHAPTER 7: DISCOVERING AND USING MEMBERS' SPIRITUAL GIFTS

1. To obtain spiritual gifts analyses, write for the *Modified Houts Questionnaire*, Charles E. Fuller Institute of Evangelism and Church Growth, Box 989, Pasadena, CA 91101. Also see "Gifts Analysis Questionnaire," pp. 125-133 from *Discover Your Gifts*, a workbook published by the Christian Reformed Home Missions, 2850 Kalamazoo Avenue, Grand Rapids, MI 49560.

2. Kennon L. Callahan, *Twelve Keys to an Effective Church* (San Francisco: Harper & Row, 1983).
3. Ibid., pp. 7-8.

CHAPTER 8: DEVELOPING THE CONGREGATION'S MISSION

1. Shawchuck and Heuser, *Leading the Congregation*, p. 212.
2. Hugh Anderson, James Cushman, Henry Snedeker-Meier, Bruce Tischler, and David Wasserman, contributors, *Congregational Mission Studies* (Louisville, KY: Evangelism and Church Development Ministry Unit, Presbyterian Church (U.S.A.), 1989), 18.01.
3. Ibid., 18.09.
4. Ibid., 18.09.
5. Carl S. Dudley, *Making the Small Church Effective* (Nashville: Abingdon Press, 1978), p. 135.
6. Ibid., p. 129.
7. For more information, see James C. Fenhagen, *Ministry and Solitude: the Ministry of the Laity and the Clergy in Church and Society* (New York: Seabury, 1981), pp. 47-48.

CHAPTER 9: CREATING CHANGES

1. Form of Government, *Book of Order*, G-10.0102i.
2. Shawchuck and Heuser, *Leading the Congregation*, p. 232.
3. Ibid., pp. 233-234. I have adapted these three variables from Shawchuck and Heuser who credit Chris Argyris and Donald A. Schön, *Theory in Practice*, (San Francisco: Jossey-Bass, 1974) for the material.
4. "On Crafting a Fundamental Change Strategy," *Transformation*, 1 (Spring 1994), p. 8.
5. The Center for Parish Development, *Classes of Changes in Church Organizations* (Chicago: The Center for Parish Development, 1989), p. 16. Used with permission.
6. See Douglas John Hall, *The Steward: A Biblical Symbol Come of Age* (Grand Rapids, MI: William B. Eerdmans Publishing Company and New York: Friendship Press, 1990).
7. See *A Sequence for Managing Church Organizational Change* (Chicago: The Center For Parish Development, 1989) for a

discussion of possible steps to effect change.

8. For a more complete discussion, see Margaret Morris, et al., *Dealing with Conflict in the Congregation* (Atlanta: Presbyterian Peacemaking Program, n.d.), pp. 4,5.

9. Norman Shawchuck, *How to Manage Conflict in the Church: Understanding and Managing Conflict* (Indianapolis, IN: Spiritual Growth Resources, 1983), I:10.

APPENDIX A

1. See Ben Campbell Johnson, *Pastoral Spirituality: A Focus for Ministry* (Philadelphia: The Westminster Press, 1988), pp. 68-76 for more background on these types.

2. The idea for this Bible study originally came from Lyman Coleman, but I have lost the source.

3. The basic model is drawn from Robert H. Ramey, Jr. & Ben Campbell Johnson, *Living the Christian Life: A Guide to Reformed Spirituality* (Louisville, KY: Westminster/John Knox Press, 1992), pp.54-55.

APPENDIX D

1. Roberta C. Bondi, *To Pray and to Love: Conversations on Prayer with the Early Church* (Minneapolis: Fortress Press, 1991), p. 14.

2. Ibid.

3. Ibid.

4. Stan Jones, "The Care & Feeding of Church Officers," *Faith at Work* (November/December 1990), p. 11.

Anderson, Hugh and James Cushman, Henry Snedeker-Meier, Bruce Tischler, and David Wasserman, contributors. *Congregational Mission Studies: Mission Studies Notebook.* Louisville, KY: Evangelism and Church Development Ministry Unit, Presbyterian Church (U.S.A.), 1989.

Anderson, James D. and Ezra Earl Jones. *The Management of Ministry.* San Francisco: Harper & Row, 1978.

Baptism, Eucharist, and Ministry. Geneva, Switzerland: World Council of Churches, 1982.

Bondi, Roberta. *To Pray & to Love: Conversations on Prayer in the Early Church.* Minneapolis: Fortress Press, 1991.

Callahan, Kennon L. *Effective Church Leadership: Building on the Twelve Keys.* San Francisco: Harper & Row, 1990.

———. *Twelve Keys to an Effective Church.* San Francisco: Harper & Row, 1983.

Campbell, Thomas C. and Gary B. Reierson. *The Gift of Administration: Theological Bases for Ministry.* Philadelphia: The Westminster Press, 1981.

Carroll, Jackson W. *As One With Authority: Reflective Leadership in Ministry.* Louisville, KY: Westminster/John Knox Press, 1991.

Carroll, Jackson W. and Carl S. Dudley and William McKinney, eds. *Handbook for Congregational Studies.* Nashville: Abingdon Press, 1986.

Dudley, Carl S. *Making the Small Church Effective.* Nashville: Abingdon Press, 1978.

Erikson, Erik H. *Childhood and Society.* New York: W. W. Norton, 1964.

Fisher, Roger & William Urey. *Getting to Yes: Negotiating Agreement Without Giving In.* New York: Penguin Books, 1983.

Foster, Richard J. *Celebration of Discipline: The Path to Spiritual Growth.* San Francisco: Harper & Row, 1978.

Greenleaf, Robert K. *Servant Leadership.* New York: Paulist Press, 1977.

Hall, Douglas John. *An Awkward Church.* Louisville, KY: Presbyterian Church (U.S.A.), 1993.

————.*The Steward: A Biblical Symbol Come of Age.* Grand Rapids, MI: William B. Eerdmans Publishing Company, and New York: Friendship Press, 1990.

Halverstadt, Hugh F. *Managing Church Conflict.* Louisville, KY: Westminster/John Knox Press, 1991.

Hanson, Paul D. *The People Called; The Growth of Community in the Bible.* San Francisco: Harper & Row, 1986.

Hauerwas, Stanley and William H. Willimon. *Resident Aliens.* Nashville: Abingdon Press, 1989.

Hopewell, James F. *Congregation: Stories and Structure.* Philadelphia: Fortress Press, 1987.

Johnson, Ben Campbell. *Pastoral Spirituality: A Focus for Ministry.* Philadelphia: The Westminster Press, 1988.

Leadership Skills for Effective Ministry. Naperville, IL: Center for Parish Development, 1980.

Leas, Speed B. *Discover Your Conflict Management Style.* Washington, D.C.: The Alban Institute, 1984.

———.*Moving Your Church Through Conflict.* Washington, D.C.: The Alban Institute, 1985.

Lewis, G. Douglass. *Resolving Church Conflicts: A Case Study Approach for Local Congregations.* San Francisco: Harper & Row, 1981.

Likert, Rensis. *The Human Organization.* New York: McGraw-Hill Book Company, 1967.

——— and Jane Gibson Likert. *New Ways of Managing Conflict.* New York: McGraw-Hill Book Company, 1976.

Lindgren, Alvin. *Let My People Go: Empowering Laity for Ministry.* Nashville: Abingdon Press, 1980.

———.*Management for Your Church: A Systems Approach.* Nashville: Abingdon Press, 1977.

Luecke, David S. and Samuel Southard. *Pastoral Administration: Integrating Ministry and Management in the Church.* Waco, TX: Word Books, 1986.

Mead, Loren B. *The Once and Future Church.* Washington, D.C.: The Alban Institute, 1991.

Minear, Paul S. *Images of the Church in the New Testament.* Philadelphia: The Westminster Press, 1960.

Morris, Margaret, et al. *Dealing with Conflict in the Congregation.* Atlanta: Presbyterian Peacemaking Program, n.d.

Oswald, Roy S. *Clergy Stress and Burnout: A Survival Kit for Church Professionals.* Minneapolis: Ministers Life Resources, 1982.

Pappas, Anthony G. *Entering the World of the Small Church: A Guide for Leaders.* Washington, D.C.: The Alban Institute, 1988.

Presbyterian Church (U.S.A.). *The Constitution of the Presbyterian Church (U.S.A.)*, Part II: *Book of Order.* Louisville, KY: Office of the General Assembly, 1994.

Ramey, Robert H. Jr. *The Minister's Role in Evangelism.* Decatur, GA: CTS Press, 1985.

———— and Ben Campbell Johnson. *Living the Christian Life: A Guide to Reformed Spirituality.* Louisville, KY: Westminster/John Knox Press, 1992.

Richards, Lawrence O. and Clyde Hoeldtke. *A Theology of Church Leadership.* Grand Rapids, MI: Zondervan Publishing House, 1981.

Shawchuck, Norman. *How to Manage Conflict in the Church: Understanding & Managing Conflict.* Naperville, IL: Center for Parish Development, 1983.

———— and Roger Heuser. *Leading the Congregation: Caring for Yourself While Serving the People.* Nashville: Abingdon Press, 1993.

A Systems Model of the Church in Ministry and Mission. Chicago: Center for Parish Development, n.d.

Theology and Worship Ministry Unit, Presbyterian Church (U.S.A.). *Growing in the Life of Christian Faith.* Louisville, KY: 1989. Also printed in the *Minutes of the 201st General Assembly (1989) of the Presbyterian Church (U.S.A.)*, Part I: Journal, pp. 467-487.

Thompson, Ernest Trice. *Through the Ages: A History of the Christian Church.* Richmond: The CLC Press, 1965.

"How can I grow as a church leader?" If you have ever asked yourself that question, this book will help you...Now more than ever we must nurture church leaders, since the church stands on a new "missionary" plain that requires us to view the world differently...Lay leaders today hunger for a deeper Christian experience and spiritually growing leaders can face the challenge of today's world.

ROBERT H. RAMEY, JR. has served as Professor of Ministry at Columbia Theological Seminary in Decatur, Georgia since 1979. Prior to that time he served five pastorates in Georgia, North Carolina, and Virginia. Educated at Hampden-Sydney College and Union Theological Seminary in Virginia, he is author of *The Minister's Role in Evangelism* and *The Cross Bearer* and co-author of *Living the Christian Life*.

ISBN 1-885121-13-X